Khamsin

KHAMSIN

Memoirs and Poetry
by a Native Israeli

Moshe Dor

An Original by Three Continents

First English Language Edition
By Three Continents Press
P.O. Box 38009
Colorado Springs, CO 80937-8009

Library of Congress Cataloging-in-Publication Data

Dor, Mosheh, 1932–
      (Selections. English. 1994)
      Khamsin: memoirs and poetry by a native Israeli / Moshe Dor.
          p. cm.
      ISBN 0-89410-763-1: $25.00 — ISBN 0-89410-764-X (pbk.): $15.00
      1. Dor, Mosheh, 1932–   —Translations into English.   2. Dor, Mosheh, 1932–
      —Biography.   3. Poets, Israeli—Biography.
      I. Title.
      PJ5054.D6A2   1994
      892.4'16–dc20
      (B)
                                                                                93-2400
                                                                                CIP
                                                                                AC

Cover Design and Art Work by Joyce Mulcahy
Works previously copyrighted are specified in acknowledgements.

Acknowledgments

Some of this work has appeared in the following publications: *Ariel*, "To the Sun" (trans. by Yael Lotan); *Confrontation*, "New Alphabet" (trans. by Barbara Goldberg); *Jewish Quarterly*, "Assimilation," "Jericho," and "Tell Me the Truth" (trans. by Barbara Goldberg); *Modern Hebrew Literature*, "Rag Doll" (trans. by Seymour Mayne); *Modern Poetry in Translation*, "Curtain" (trans. by Seymour Mayne); *Parchment*, "Decision" and "Russian Doll" (trans. by Seymour Mayne); *Poet Lore*, "Basic Vocabulary" (trans. by Catherine Harnett Shaw), "Orangutan," and "Without Commitments" (trans. by Elaine Magarrell); *Prairie Schooner*, "Anti-Abstract Poem" and "Bruise" (trans. by Barbara Goldberg); *Tel Aviv Review*, "Goliath" and "Shelter" (trans. by Barbara Goldberg); and *Translation*, "Cleaving" (trans. by Laura Fargas), "In Kaestner's Footsteps" (trans. by Marilyn Millstone), "December," "Goliath," "Shampoo," and "The Art of Waiting" (trans. by Barbara Goldberg).

I am deeply grateful to my translators who gave so generously of their time and spirit: Cicely Angleton, Laura Fargas, Barbara Goldberg, Eva Greene, Merrill Leffler, Yael Lotan, Elaine Magarrell, Seymour Mayne, Marilyn Millstone, James Oppenheim, Mitchell Roberson, Catherine Harnett Shaw, Myra Sklarew, and Henry Taylor. I am especially grateful to Barbara Goldberg, without whose vision, energy, and editing skills this book would not have been possible.

Six poems were just accepted by the *Webster Review*, "Town," translated by Laura Fargas; "Shelter" and "Balance of Power," translated by Barbara Goldberg; "Magnets," translated by Catherine Harnett Shaw; "Time Zones," translated by Elaine Magarrell; and "Circe," translated by Henry Taylor.

All memoirs and poems with the exception of "To the Sun," were translated with the author.

Table of Contents

Preface

This is the age of exile. Within the boundaries of homeland we dream of escape. And when we have gone out of the land, we cannot breathe in the new atmosphere; we long for homeland.

For some, exile is imposed from without: war, famine, an untenable political regime, overwhelming pressure from the state whose requirements come before the individual's, including the sacrifice of sons and daughters.

And when the exile is not geographical, like that of the Marranos[1], the one in exile appears to observe the outward norms all the while clinging to a people or a language, to the values and shared memories of a lost world which holds sway over him.

Or as Moshe Dor writes in *Khamsin* (a hot desert wind originating in the Sahara, so intense as to alter perception of color and light), "Poets go into exile from interior exile . . . the land of exile is the motherland." Or in his poem "Town":

> The town of my birth is the town where
> I live, my guarantee against the anxieties
> of immigrants . . .
>
> Why, then, when the mulberries
> unscroll their sticky bright sprouts
> am I filled with nostalgia for towns
> where I wasn't born, won't ever live?

---

[1]Jewish inhabitants of Moorish Spain who converted to Christianity during the Middle Ages but who continued secretly to observe Judaism.

This exile lends to the poet's voice the anguish of dislocation, resignation, longing, and irony. He looks in from the outside, though he exists in the center of the fire. Like the dreamer who is both observing and observed, the poet is the central actor and audience at the same instant. He negotiates the distance between the two like one who swims for his life in a turbulent sea.

And how is it to live in this condition? In "Shelter," Moshe Dor writes:

> We cleaned out the bomb shelter,
> a municipal edict too stringent
> to ignore. We worked diligently:
> . . .
>
>   Now we can wait
> for evil from any direction. Only
> our image reflected in that sliver
> of mirror is slightly blurred, perhaps
> because we have let down our guard.

A prophetic poem—witness the SCUD missiles not long ago volleying forth to Israel from Iraq's western fringe—filled with the longing for normality, with what it means to live on the edge.

Vigilance: perhaps that is the lodestone of these poems. Behind Israel's struggle for and achievement of the kind of life we, in more neutral territory, take for granted is that eye, always open. To live that way for one's whole life exacts an extraordinary price.

It is said that God is like the fish of the sea, with eyes always open. But it is not God's domain that requires vigilance. It is man's: this homeland which Moshe Dor is made from, this wilderness. This oasis that is the land of Israel, this sea made in the shape of a harp. These mountains. These stones into which the sun pours its life. And out of which light goes back into the atmosphere. He is made of this land and it infuses every poem he writes.

In "Identifying Marks," the poet asks why Byzantium has fallen when it could have survived a siege with its "granaries . . . overflowing, / the walls" which "might have borne the impact / of Turkish cannonballs." And there is even the rumor of rescue by the Italians. Ah, how well we know about one country looking after another! "How to explain the metropolis' fall," he writes. "Historians say one small gate was left unlatched, perhaps / from simple oversight. Through that gate / the Sultan's force penetrated the city."

In every image does the force of history ignite. Though it is Byzantium, we remember Herod's fortress and the mass suicide of the Hebrews, we remember the fall of Jerusalem and the exile to Babylon, the lament of Jeremiah. On neutral territory, centuries later, the poet examines the shards of defeat: Constantine's "purple sandals" by which his corpse is identified.

"One small gate . . . left unlatched": doors, gates, these are Israel's trademarks—Mea Shearim, the place of 100 gates; the golden gate sealed until resurrection; Jaffa gate; the Dung gate; the gates of the Kabalah. Ancient and modern, entwined. And the poignancy, the impossibility of salvation from enemies through the use of gates, the irony of airborne missiles, air which heretofore carried the likes of Ezekiel or the signs of covenant.

Here are poems which explore the terror of the creative act for "what would ripen, like / a terrible fetus," poems in which skinheads inhabit the same space as Orpheus but cannot hear him. And here is the language: "I . . . fortify myself behind 22 protective fences / *aleph, bet, gimmel.*" And our companions, found and lost: "No, it will not be I traversing the brambles of your sleep / to lead the caravan. / Earth is stronger."

Here, not only the son in exile but the motherland too is submerged: "I think tomorrow, / surely by the day after, / the signal to return will come / from the drowned motherland." In a memoir written during the celebration of Tel Aviv's birthday, the son cannot find his city for the changes: "The little houses have disappeared. The bells of the camels' long necks are silent. The horizon is hidden behind tall buildings. My Tel Aviv is hiding . . . She hides, and I seek her, in love and despair."

Here, the struggle for speech so that it may be offered in love, "I breath effortlessly / and lead an infinite column / of words, all clearly enunciated / . . . to create / the alphabet anew so that I / may utter now to you, *Beloved.*"

And here, in memoirs, we find a kind of *Künstlerroman*, the writer protagonist in a life and death struggle toward maturity and his artistic mission, a form most unusual among Israeli writers and particularly important in the way it documents the parallel struggle of Israel's rebirth and maturation.

Vigilance. The land. Language and history. The power of love. Exile. A boy who tears at the wild vines which entrap him, like the ram of Abraham caught in the thicket. Escape and return. The soul of a man struggling between the outlines of his life and the life of his nation whose days and nights mingle in a vortex of Biblical proportions: Moshe Dor, *Khamsin*.

Myra Sklarew

Part One

Prose:
This Parched Land

To the Sun

In the early 1930s Tel Aviv was a little white town and the gleaming sands of gold fell in bewitching folds toward the sea, which was a vast haven between blue and green. The coarse *zifzif* sand rustled under one's bare toes. Camel caravans passed, bells clanging on their swaying necks. The Moslem cemetery was a mystery where fearful possibilities lurked among the tombstones. Wild vines clothed the hills.

Beyond the Workers' Quarter, which was strewn with tiny houses set in gardens, stretched a desert of white sand. Out there stood a solitary lamp post like a lighthouse. In the long summer evenings the lamp cast long shadows on the sand. Children would sit around it, telling stories. A few paces away, moon flowers grew on the hummocks. It was generally believed that the flowers opened in the moonlight, and that their pollen was bad for the eyes.

On Keren Kayemet Boulevard wind-struck tamarisks sheltered faded benches. People would respectfully point out Ben Gurion's house. And it was not unusual to see Paula Ben Gurion standing at her gate, to waylay women friends on their way to and from the grocery. In her far-from-polished language she would express strong opinions on the contents of their baskets, or on more elevated subjects.

Hadassah Park adjoined the zoo. It was a refuge for lovers and the love-hungry. The air was filled with sighs. The plants grew wild and the dusky growth lent wings to adolescent fantasy. North of here flowed the Yarkon, with eucalyptus trees rising on its banks. To go all the way up to "The Seven Mills" was to have high adventure. The river was a deep green and mothers forbade bathing in it for fear of *bilharzia*. But those who knew such things said that at the mouth of the river the seawater neutralized the bacteria.

Two magnificent sycamores grew in our yard. By day birds held a permanent celebration in their branches. By night bats glided to and from the tops, and woe to him or her in whose hair the creatures became entangled, as popular belief had it. The sycamores spread a tremendous green canopy over the sand, their roots twisting endlessly, their fruit falling all around, sticky, wormy, and bird-pecked. They were a kingdom in themselves, and an imaginative child could find all his heart's desire under them—an ant-lion's nest, red oleander petals on a ground moistened by a slowly dripping tap, a bunch of twigs, a handful of shells.

In our neighborhood people fervently read the workers' newspapers, rallied to the call of the Hagana, sent their children to the pioneer youth movements and later to the labor settlements and the Palmach. In our neighborhood working people lived modest lives and clung to the ideals of their youth, even when their hair was sprinkled with gray.

Years later I came upon a poem by Avigdor Hameiri—a torn, seething soul, reeling with talent and a burning injustice—"Believing Again":

> Sun-dazzles laughingly toy with me,
> The scent of jasmine greets me by surprise:
> I believe again.
>
> A baby smiling from the sea blue—
> And once again I want to be, to dream,
> Right here on earth.
>
> The heat is woman's heat. The air is sweet.
> One of my enemies approaches,
> Bids me good day.
>
> Wonder sinks deep, deep into me.
> The houses of Tel Aviv are all aquiver:
> Fairyland castles.
>
> A ship of immigrants beckons from afar,
> And once again upon me smiles
> God's countenance from the sky.

Soon lawless love will burst forth here.
I stop my blood, my pounding heart,
And I await.

Sweet faith clings to me lovingly.
To me the golden sand is singing. My heart subsides.
And I sleep.

In my Tel Aviv childhood there were many painful days. I don't wish
to pretty them up out of rueful nostalgia. Whoever finds it hard to
accept things as they are, to be swallowed in the rank and file, to
repeat clichés without a qualm, whomever fate has cursed with a
"difficult" personality, must expect to suffer. Nevertheless, Hameiri's
poem expresses that dreamy Tel Aviv that now and then sheltered
even "difficult" sons under her wing. She is no more. Hameiri's fairy-
land castles, sweetly quivering, glow only in Nachum Gutman's paint-
ings.

The little houses have disappeared. The bells on the camels' long
necks are silent. The horizon is hidden behind tall buildings. The syca-
mores have been cut down. The air is polluted and the water of the
Yarkon is tainted with effluence. My Tel Aviv is hiding. God's coun-
tenance does not smile down on me from a sky that is lower than it
used to be.

She hides, and I seek her, in love and despair. Through jammed
streets poisoned with gasoline fumes I stalk the scent of jasmine that
has fled down bluish tunnels: I know I can never reach it. But from the
sycamores a storm of birds bursts out, boldly, gloriously, toward the sun.

Translated by Yael Lotan

Coals in the Mouth

"Stuttering": A speech impediment in which the speaker stops and is obstructed in the flow of his speaking when trying to articulate certain syllables, or despite himself repeats one syllable several times . . . Stuttering as psychoneurosis develops in children inclined to an exaggerated sensitivity and mental instability. Supporters of the "mental" theory regard stuttering as a phenomenon of fear, which causes a reaction of anxious extra-tension, anticipating impeded speech and endeavoring to avoid its unwelcome results.

There is a theory which establishes . . . lessening tension in the stutterer as the primary goal. One shouldn't be coerced to avoid stuttering but should be eased in stuttering . . . . When one is rid of the incessant panic to avoid stuttering, the mental tension grows less and possibilities present themselves for psychotherapeutical treatment.

The Hebrew Encyclopedia

And Moses said unto the Lord . . . but I am slow of speech and of a slow tongue.

Exodus 4:10

When did I become slow of speech? Certainly not in the first years of life. I don't recall having any speech impediment until fourth or fifth grade. Then stuttering dealt me a tremendous blow. Years later, I would read that speech impediments, if not caused by a physical malformation, were the result of psychological stress. I'm sure I was under such stress when my lips refused to properly shape various words. I have no doubt either that the stress grew greater and greater after I began stuttering, a vicious circle for a child who knew no way to escape.

In the secret depths of my heart I knew the reason for the stress, but I wouldn't admit to it. In those days, we had no IQ tests, and perhaps such tests were simply unknown to the tiny community of psychologists practicing in the land of Israel in the early 1940s. There was, however, a psychological counseling service in Tel Aviv, directed by a Professor Schneurson, and one day my parents took me to him. Even in my first days at elementary school, it was clear to them that my intellectual development was above average; probably my teacher told them I languished in class, bored to death with the assigned studies.

Professor Schneurson confirmed their perceptions. Among other things, my reading ability was years ahead of my classmates'. Maybe there were other clues; I don't know. Anyway, I was skipped from second into third grade. Shortly afterward, the school wanted to skip me again, but my parents refused. Not that they had any training in child psychology, but somehow they grasped on their own the burdens inherent in skipping a class, obliging the child to struggle with older kids. They adamantly refused to widen the gap that already existed between me and other children.

Even with only one skipped grade, I had a constant, unrelenting struggle to maintain my position in the class hierarchy. It wasn't enough to be smart. I needed to acquire additional qualities to stay in the race for the girls' favor. Unfortunately, in that area I was destined to occupy an inferior position.

In spite of looking rather nice—my mother used to tell a story about the actress Chana Robina, the shining light of the Habima Theater, stopping my pram to kiss my fair curls—I lagged behind my friends in simple physical skills. Given the difference in age, I suppose it was inevitable, but the older I grew, the more serious that difference seemed. I had to compensate for the age difference by constantly radiating an intellectual glow. My wit became famous, and so did my creative imagination. But who can guess the level of psychological energy I poured into igniting my endless fireworks?

On top of the "stress" at school, there was "stress" at home. By nature, I was never enthusiastic about the usual entertainments of childhood. I preferred to read and meditate. Not that I was completely detached from the neighborhood kids—sometimes I played in the improvised soccer games or joined the gatherings around our solitary electric pole, which stood in splendid isolation amid the dunes. On the whole, though, I was much more interested in my books and my thoughts. The other children were quick to pick up on this, and reacted pitilessly to my aloofness.

The reaction at home to my "alienation" was just as bad. That term didn't exist yet in Hebrew, but the perception was clear nevertheless. My family demanded, in so many words, that I be "like all the others." My parents understood that I was intellectually precocious, but refused to accept what that meant in everyday life. They thought that if I spent more time with friends, like "a normal kid," instead of habitually disappearing to some hide-out with a bunch of books, everything would turn out terrific and I would be both "gifted" and "okay." This desperate wish that their son be "just like everybody else" hung like a sword over their heads and mine until our family framework finally crumbled. This isn't the place to enumerate the excruciating pains involved in that collapse; suffice it to say they were many and dreadful.

Sometime during that period, beset by both internal and external stress, I reached the stage where the organs of speech revolted. I can't remember whether it happened gradually or all at once, but the fact is that my stuttering struck me brutally in both places, home and school. But if at school my classmates and teachers came to accept it, learning to see it as a symptom to be understood and not mocked (although this was a major adjustment which took some time), at home my stuttering became a source of perennial bitterness.

My condition was not a permanent state of stammering but an occasional one, a sort of seismograph of rising or receding tension. Quite often the day would pass uneventfully; my speech would be fluent and comprehensible both in school—where I kept my position at the top of the class—and at home. Once tension mounted, though, no matter what its source, my stuttering instantly re-emerged. The tongue became slow, each lip became wooden. Certain letters, always more difficult to pronounce, became impossible to articulate. Even the easy letters would stumble on my lips.

Not surprisingly, I became a wizard at finding clever ways to avoid public speaking or readings, while my written assignments, particularly the literary compositions, became more and more fluent. Slipping away to write was for me not only the result of my creative energy growing stronger and steadier, but also the result of self-defense. My writing,

lauded by the teacher and applauded by the class, was a way to circum-
navigate the need for speech.

At school, once my dire situation became clear, the teacher would
spare me the ordeal and himself read my essays to the class for the
edification of all. But at home? Who could express the intensity of
despair that choked the stutterer and his immediate circle of listeners,
his own flesh and blood, when his affliction became strident? Who
could describe the world fracturing around him? My parents, who by
then were supposed to be richly equipped to "understand the child's
psyche," and especially "the problem child's psyche," sometimes dis-
played a frank impatience with my "problem." Meanwhile my sister,
seven years older than me, used my "defect" as a deadly weapon in her
quest for primacy in our family. She'd make up and sing "funny" songs,
songs that echoed the various forms of my speech impediment. Her
verses were bad and her rhyming faulty, but the barbs went home. I
would feel the exposed flesh of my soul smarting for a long time after
one of her musical fusillades.

At school the full, humiliating extent of my predicament was ex-
posed in one terrible event, which was followed by the discovery of a
golden compromise without which the human race (in the form of me)
could not have survived. It would be far-fetched to call my class tutor,
veteran teacher that he was, a man gifted with extraordinary pedagogi-
cal subtlety, but neither was he a fool. Indeed, I don't know why he
hadn't managed before then to receive the stuttering signals broadcast
in his direction, but on this occasion they became ineluctable.

On the fateful day, he asked each student in turn to read some
verses from the Bible aloud—I can't recall whether it was one of the
prophets, or maybe a chapter of historiography. When my turn came,
I simply refused. No embellishments or explanations, just a refusal. The
silence in the classroom was thick enough to cut with a knife. Drops
of sweat covered my brow and my heart pounded in my chest. It was
probably one of those days predestined to founder on some hidden reef,
when a child wakes up with a clear sense that something bad is going
to happen to him soon.

Did the day start with a family fight? Or did that ominous tension
start rising like a dark wave at school? At that moment, one thing was
transcendentally clear to me: I couldn't obey the teacher without the
disgrace of my faulty speech becoming the property of the whole world,
so that I would be cloaked in shame forever. If only the earth would

split open and swallow me before the horrible thing happened!

With extreme difficulty I managed to utter the tiny word "no." Then I sank back into an opaque silence with not even a small chink in its gray armor. The teacher couldn't understand my strange obstinacy, and repeated his demand that I read my verses again and again. I just kept shaking my head, "no." The feelings shining out from my classmates' faces ranged from malicious joy to deep compassion. Finally, the teacher ordered me to leave the room and not to come back without bringing at least one of my parents along. Obviously he'd concluded that I'd gone out of my young mind.

I got up and walked out against a background of profound, unbearable silence. I remember it was a bright, transparent summer day. Our school faced the sea, the sun's glaring light thrown off its blue-green expanses in sparks of incandescent copper. My shirt was completely damp with sweat and heavy drops were running down my pale face. My eyes were dry and smarting: I was far beyond tears.

I didn't go back to school for days. Immediately after I had left the room, some of my classmates volunteered to the teacher why I had behaved as I did. Let it be said to his credit that he instantly understood the enormity of his error and contacted my parents, specifically my mother. (At that time, my father had a job in another town, and wasn't able to come home more than two weekends a month.) I don't know what was said between them, but afterward my teacher scrupulously avoided putting me to any similar test. I went on being one of the best students in my class all the way to graduation, and the extreme variations in the quality of my speech didn't affect my standing.

As it happened, our school was affiliated with a teachers' seminary, whose students—all of them girls—would occasionally grace us with an "exemplary class," as their curriculum required. Because I had the reputation of being especially erudite in history and literature, my sister's classmates (she was studying for a teacher's license at that very school) would beg her to persuade me to deal mercifully with them when their turn came to teach an "exemplary class." It was well known that I could destroy a tender young student teacher with learned comments based on my knowledge of remote Hebrew writers and the minutest details of conspiracies hatched in the bedrooms of medieval European palaces. Sometimes the class tutor himself—he taught us most of the humanities—would ask me confidentially to demonstrate my erudition "in a positive way" when the guest teacher happened to be a favorite of his, or when the principal popped in to inspect the quality of our studying. Or was it the quality of his teaching? That would remain a mystery. You may assume that when "showing off" I didn't suffer from any speech impediment. During these hours of grace my demon would be totally exorcised, as if it were only a nightmare fading away at the first crack of dawn.

The stuttering trauma still haunted me in high school. There, too, I had to endure open confrontations with several teachers in order to make my predicament clear. Since I was one of the best students in the school, the saving compromises were again reached. My essays were considered exemplary by the teachers of Hebrew and world literature; my historical erudition had no competitors. In English language and literature I was again one of the very best. The teachers, or at least the more intelligent among them, found effective ways to get the best from me without making me trip over the hurdles of my redundant speech. Still, my stuttering remained variable, and often I didn't stammer at all.

I fought alone in my war against the "slowness of tongue." I don't know why, but I never received treatment, and that lonely war cost much anguish, scarring me for life. Eventually I managed to overcome most obstacles unless I was extremely tired, or extremely stressed, somehow pushed beyond endurance. I think I'm entitled to say that in order to re-acquire a norm of reasonably fluent speech—and even the ability to make public speeches—I had no alternative but to smash my speaking tools and then rebuild them from the very beginning.

Moshe (Moses), the son of Amram, was, as the Bible says, slow of speech and of a slow tongue. In our Sources we have a beautiful fable about the child Moses stretching his hand toward the gold that the Pharaoh offers as the final test of whether to kill or spare him; the angel of God slaps his hand and causes Moses to take up the coals, proving by that gesture that he is stupid and not to be feared. Moses filled his mouth with burning coals and maimed himself for life, becoming a stutterer. I could never read that ancient tale without a choking feeling of intense identification with my great namesake.

Even now I find it impossible to listen indifferently to—let alone enjoy—jokes about stuttering. The blade lacerates my own flesh. *And the Lord said unto him . . . Is not Aaron the Levite thy brother? I know that he can speak well . . . And he shall be thy spokesman unto the people: and he shall be, even he shall be to thee instead of a mouth . . .*

I wasn't so lucky. I had neither Aaron, nor any other brother, to serve as my mouth. I write this not out of self pity, but because I want to state a fact, one which I had no choice but to experience in all its terror and to battle in a lonely, cruel, and tormented struggle, a struggle that will end only with life itself.

Translated by Laura Fargas

The Escape

Biographies are only man's garments and buttons. It's impossible to write one's own biography.

Mark Twain, *Autobiography*

Neither a garment nor a button . . . only sand.

Once when I was a child, I escaped from home. Where could I go? Even as I ran away, a sense of futility rose in me. I ran wildly down a road of sand, my eyes burning with unshed tears. Past a solitary electric pole I turned westward to the sea, following one sandy road after another.

I reached the hills of the beach, where wild vines entwined on the sand. On the bright golden hills, the sun had closed the moon flowers, storing their blinding pollen within their petals. The sun filled the whole land.

At the top of the hill I felt how mercilessly the sand scorched my bare feet. Below the slope lay a vast ocean of shifting colors, lucid green deepening to dark blue.

Why did I run away? I don't remember. Insults to children are not measured or recorded.

Gliding down to the cool beach, I pushed my scorched feet into the cool gravel, and the burning subsided. My lungs filled with salty air, smelling faintly of iodine. I heard a distant ringing of bells that vibrated on the air and faded away.

I was alone. The shallow water softly rustled. I knew I would return home defeated. The sun placed a crown of fire, tight as a vise, on my head. I poured seawater on it, which quickly evaporated, leaving droplets of salt in my hair.

Among the green algae-covered rocks, the water formed little pools. Transparent, tiny fish danced in them. Crabs were running on the beach, leaving traces of miniature feet before diving into their holes. Myriad shells lay around.

With burning eyes I gazed at the horizon. The sea was mine, my coat of many colors. I remembered the boy Joseph whom jealous brothers threw into a pit. But I had no brothers.

Watery sand passed through my fingers and dried into towers and battlements, drop by drop, level upon level. As the tower rose it narrowed, began to sag, and finally collapsed in ruins.

I collected rare shells, convoluted and conch-like, spotted and striped, pure and pink like virgin flesh. I crammed them into my pockets, and then, crushed by a grief too heavy to support, took them out and threw them away. Only splints of shells and moist grains of sand remained in my pockets.

Impartial, warm, and clear time flowed in the arteries of my life, what had been and what was going to be.

And the rough places were made plain.[1] The asphalt buried the sand, and the horizon was devoured by the jaws of big buildings. And the sun wasted immense energy on the polluted water of the sea, the coat of many colors of the beloved son who had been sold to the Ishmaelites.

I traced my steps back, walking slowly. A terrible burden weighed on my shoulders. As I climbed the sand hills, the wild vines caught my legs and I pulled them out, tearing the vines. The moon flowers were emerging toward the sunset out of their yellow lampshades. I turned my eyes away lest the evil powder enter and blind them. Past the solitary electric pole, from sand street to sand street, I walked home.

In order to escape again, and to return.

Neither garment nor button.

Not even sand.

Translated by Eva Greene

---

[1]Isaiah 40:4

The Friend

In faraway days of a huge sun and a mythological sea, my parents decided to send me to a kibbutz.

I don't know who gave them that advice. In those years, the first years of World War II, my father worked in Haifa and came home only on weekends, once every few weeks. The burden of managing the household and keeping the family together fell on my mother's shoulders. She was obsessed with cleanliness and invested prodigious energy in polishing the little house in Workers' Quarter B in northern Tel Aviv. She'd wash the floors, even the outside stairs leading up to the house, and dust the few pieces of furniture, particularly the piano my sister played. The good Lord knows where the money for that piano came from: my father's wages didn't suffice for our up-keep, and out of the three rooms of the house, one, the smallest, was regularly rented, the lodger changing every few years. But my sister's piano teachers predicted a great future for her, and whenever she returned from her studies at the Teachers' College, she practiced on the piano. She loved that piano and nobody paid attention to my complaints that she played some pieces of music so repetitiously that they made me sick.

So who advised them to give me a taste of collective life? Somebody from the Tel Aviv Psychological Service for Municipal Schools? Friends of my parents? Teachers? I was about ten or eleven years old at that time, a model student, and also a voracious reader, spending most of my time with books—indeed, far too much for my own good according to my betters. Instead of horsing around with friends, I preferred reading *Treasure Island* or *King Solomon's Mines* and daydreaming. And of course there was my stuttering. Indeed, I was a problem child.

The kibbutz was then not only the spearhead of proletarian

ideology, the pride of Israeli labor, but also a laboratory of pedagogical experiments. The collective settlements absorbed "outside children" of all sorts, either sent there under the auspices of national expediency—immigrant children who arrived without their families—or out of local necessity—children of divorced parents. Naturally, the "youth groups" of the kibbutz were paid for taking care of those children—they couldn't possibly sustain them on their own—either by the Jewish Agency or by private sources.

How could my parents support me? It seems that riddle had an unexpected solution.

For several years my family rented the small room in our house to a man named Ramati, who also became a close friend. Like my parents, he arrived in the country from White Russia with the third *aliya*, and like them he was a pioneer, building roads and draining swamps. For obscure reasons, Ramati moved from his original kibbutz to Tel Aviv working at various odd jobs. He wasn't married and had no children. Our family took him in. He was a kind man and loved me with all his heart, boasting of my real or imagined gifts as if I were his own son. When still very young, I used to straddle big volumes of literary and ideological magazines from my parents' library and, emitting the sound of an engine, travel from room to room. It seems to me now, after so many years, that the literary magazines were bound in yellowish, sandy colors while the ideological ones were bound in dark green. Thus I had two kinds of buses, which I changed according to whim, traveling immense distances in my imagination. Ramati claimed that the wisdom I acquired via my butt was more profound than that acquired by certain friends of his via their heads.

Ramati was no longer our lodger when my family discussed my future and what would be the best way to integrate me into children's society before I became an utter recluse. At some point he had decided to revive his former glory and joined a kibbutz in the Valley of Jezreel. Whenever he came to town he made a point to pay us a visit and always brought me a small present. I needed no proof that Ramati still loved me. He kept his bachelor status in the kibbutz, his various girl-friends being unable to hook him, claiming that he had grown so used to his independence he couldn't possibly exchange it even for all the delights of marriage. Anyway, Ramati actively participated in the discussions about me, and quite possibly it was he who brought forth the kibbutz idea. The collective society had had impressive successes in the education of children and youth and Ramati spoke warmly of the high quality and far-reaching achievements of kibbutz education. Gradually, he would introduce me to the Society of Children, taking into consideration my excessive sensitivity. He recited from Proverbs: "Raise a child in the way he should go: and when he is old, he will not depart from it." He would accompany me every step of the way, like a father-trainer, and would smooth all obstacles. The mere innovation of kibbutz life, in the bosom of nature; the animals, the trips, the responsibility vested in the hands of the children themselves, enabling them to manage, to a respectable extent, their own lives and households; all this was bound to captivate me. Books, Ramati said, could also be found at the kibbutz.

Nobody asked me for my opinion. I knew that Ramati had invited me to visit him at his kibbutz, but I didn't have the faintest notion— not consciously—that plots were being hatched to remove me from my home and birthplace. Ramati loved me and I fully reciprocated. I thought of him, during the time he stayed with us, as the kindest of uncles, and each of his visits fortified that feeling.

And so it happened that once upon a bright morning—the Israeli sun was already gloriously shining in a blue, transparent sky—Ramati and I got up and set on our way to the Valley. My few clothes were packed in a small, battered suitcase. Was my father present at our departure? How did my mother and sister bid me farewell? Did I finally suspect the "visit" was not so innocent? I don't remember. The trip itself filled me with impressions, which dulled any despondent thoughts.

The journey from Tel Aviv to the Valley settlements was then quite a lengthy affair and we stopped along the way to drink bubbling soft drinks and eat sandwiches. I particularly remember Ramati's gray peaked cap. Each of those details was important and interesting on its own, not to mention the changing landscape and the assortment of characters on the bus. Finally we arrived. We got off the bus and began marching on a dirt road. The soil was heavy and black with big, furrowed clods. A sharp smell of manure filled my nostrils, and the lowing of cows reached my ears. We went past an orchard, the trees heavily laden with oranges. Ramati wanted to carry my suitcase, but I insisted on holding it, perhaps sensing that it was a link to what had been my previous life.

Ramati's room at the kibbutz was small and clean. It had a wardrobe, a simple bed close to the wall, and a few shelves loaded with books and newspapers. Close to another wall was a folding bed, presumably for me. And on the wall hung Van Gogh's *Sunflowers*, an extremely popular painting in those days.

Ramati treated me with utmost consideration. He did not press me into doing anything I didn't want to do. He was an exemplary liberal. I went with him to the communal dining hall for meals, which were primarily meant to satiate hunger, not to astound by culinary genius. He introduced me to several adult members, but I don't think we shared more than the usual banalities exchanged on such occasions. He also tried to acquaint me with the kibbutz children my own age, and induce me, most pleasantly as was typical of him, to take the first steps toward admittance to the Society of Children. To no avail. They didn't display any interest in me beyond that involved in a brief, noncommital encounter, and I refused to join them. Ramati didn't push me. He took me to the kibbutz library. My eyes lit up. Here there were books and I immediately felt relief. While Ramati worked I'd spend my time at the library till he arrived to pick me up for meals. I don't know what he told the librarian, but she treated me with kindness and let me browse to my heart's content, and even recommended certain titles. It's difficult for me now to judge her literary tastes, but I'm sure I had no ground for complaint.

Sometimes I'd wander the kibbutz trails, taking in the sights and sounds and smells. The odor of manure and fresh hay was the strongest. When it grew hotter I'd find shelter in the orchard, in the green dense shade of the orange trees. Sometimes, when nobody was in sight, and I was sure I was absolutely alone, I would cry. I told Ramati I wanted to go back home. He asked me to wait a few more days. Perhaps he wrote to my parents. The collective life flowed around me and didn't touch me. The values, so thoroughly talked and written about, remained—at least from my point of view—a perfectly sealed book.

I had begun to suspect that something unsavory was hidden behind the facade of that "visit." From time to time Ramati tried to bring me to parties at the Society of Children and to Sabbath receptions. I sat to the side, taking no part, covered with a heavy silence, which gradually grew heavier. When he got to his feet, I did the same. When he went away, I joined him. He neither protested nor insisted. Only his eyes became sadder.

My departure probably would have happened sooner or later, but then a true outsider arrived, a boy sent there because of serious family reasons. I don't remember his name, only a vague outline of his appearance: about my age, thin, dark-eyed, wearing short khaki pants. Ramati discovered him almost immediately on his arrival. He had a sudden inspiration, understanding our common denominator: shyness of crowds, and a difficulty—or, at the worst, an inability—to integrate into society. Immediately he introduced us to each other.

Something astonishing happened. The surroundings were no longer alien. We talked incessantly, hurriedly, jumping from topic to topic. The most understanding, tolerant adult is no substitute for a friend your own age. I led my new friend, with a surprising sense of ownership, to the communal dining hall, the orchard, the library, the children's zoological corner, the cowshed. I pointed with my hand, explained, laughed. I didn't stutter at all. The kibbutz was no longer foreign territory, but began to feel like home.

I also showed him the irrigation pool. To me it seemed very large, like a pond. The water was murky because of the muddy bottom, but it was possible to swim, to splash, to make waves. As a Tel Avivan born and raised near the sea, I knew how to swim. I had taught myself to do a clumsy, though serviceable, crawl. Several times, when gliding into the water over the muddy bank, I found my legs stuck in the mud and needed all my strength to heave them out. But a few strokes brought me to deeper water.

I liked the irrigation pool. I used to go there in my swimming trunks and, during the hottest hours of the day when the pool was deserted, I'd wade in. I don't recall being warned of any danger.

My new friend probably came from Jerusalem, and therefore didn't know how to swim. But I didn't think of that at all. How many days did that joy of meeting a soulmate last?

Perhaps it was written that the kibbutz wouldn't ever embrace me. How did my new friend arrive, on that disastrous day, at the irrigation pool? How did he drown in it? Did he come alone, or with other children—because he, without a Ramati to shield him, surely was joined to such a group—in the Society of Children? Was I present? And if not, how did I learn of the catastrophe?

Who told me?

For a long time after, nightmares haunted me. I would see the thin body struggling in the water, only his light khaki pants flickering in the darkness. The eyes, the drowning eyes, were filled with a horror and the open mouth was soundlessly screaming.

The consciousness of the end was bitter and cruel. It hit me straight in the face. I had heard people at home talking about death, about the deaths of close friends or relatives. I read of death in the newspapers, in stories. The word meant nothing but soared above me like a dark bird which never alighted on the branches.

Was I to blame?

The outcome was inevitable. I couldn't stay any longer in that place, not even for one unnecessary moment. Probably I was in shock. I demanded that Ramati send me home—immediately. All the fears gnawing at my psyche, pushed to some remote corner—fears of being exiled to the kibbutz, far from my true habitat—were released. The kibbutz now seemed like a penal colony, and I had to escape before I was doomed forever.

I returned to Tel Aviv in a bus. I went away like I came, clutching the handle of my little suitcase.

I was silent the whole way back. When I approached my house I heard the familiar piano. My life was waiting for me, hoarding both the bitter and the sweet that were allotted to me. The summer beat pitilessly on my bare head. Mounting the cement stairs, so recently washed, I felt the burning heat through my sandals. The piano sounds stopped at once.

The enormous sea rustled beyond the dunes. At night I sobbed in my sleep, and would for many nights to come.

Ramati vanished from my life. I never saw him again.

Translated by Mitchell Roberson

Cleaving

Early mental maturity isn't necessarily matched by equally precocious physical development. What is mental maturity, anyway? A readiness to accept life with all its quirks and turnings? To challenge it? To be able to decode and analyze all the phenomena that cross our paths? Or to ignore them, closing ourselves in bubbles of idiosyncratic identity that refuse to float in the current?

And what, for that matter, is physical maturity? When does the body reach a ripeness that makes it full grown? With the first sexual experience that reaches beyond onanism and enters the territory where the two sexes conjoin?

I've told how I outpaced most of my friends in vocabulary, literature, and history, even though these friends were usually older than I. My IQ, had there been IQ tests in those far off days, would probably have been higher than theirs. But in learning about intimacy, I lagged way behind. There was a simple reason for this. The girls—no matter how much they might respect my lambent intellect, my wit, my staggering erudition—preferred the older boys, who were taller and stronger, when they found themselves inclined toward romance.

What I didn't lack was desire. My cravings haunted me day and night and spun themselves into intricate fantasies, focusing on the more developed girls in my class and pioneer youth movement. At that time, I didn't know what Tolstoy had known—or so he claimed in his famous conversations with Gorky in the Crimea—that every girl of fifteen longs to sleep with a man. Tolstoy could test that theory in practice, taking advantage of the young serf girls. But in the Palestine of the early 1940s, what could I do?

Back to those years when overt sexual desire was still secreted in the depths of my consciousness. I was ten, maybe eleven. At that time

General Anders' Polish troops arrived in the Land of Israel. These soldiers had already traveled thousands of miles without ever fighting a battle.

It happened like this: the Soviet army occupied eastern Poland in the fall of 1939, as stipulated by the Ribbentrop-Molotov pact. Multitudes of fresh Polish recruits were taken prisoner. Originally, they had been intended to hold the Polish-Soviet border while the other half of Poland's army fought the Nazis. Stalin sent these Poles to camps in central Asia, but when the Germans invaded the Soviet Union, a new accord between Stalin and the exiled Polish government in London stood this arrangement on its head. Now the Soviets and the Poles were allies. Churchill persuaded Stalin to free the interned Polish soldiers, let them reorganize into military units, and leave Soviet territory in order to rejoin the struggle against Hitler under British command.

The Polish commander-in-chief, General Anders, was fanatically anti-communist, but his capacity for hatred was not exhausted on the Soviet Union. He was also a rabid anti-semite. This didn't prevent the British from evacuating Anders' troops to the Middle East and encamping them in, of all places, the Land of Israel for a period of recuperation and retraining prior to transfer to the western desert front. The Jewish soldiers among those Polish troops, sick of the traditional Jew-baiting, lost no time in deserting. They vanished into the local populace almost immediately on their arrival in Palestine.

The remaining soldiers were issued Polish uniforms, which were actually British uniforms with Polish identifying tags sewn on. The officers, though, had distinct peaked Polish army caps with the white eagle emblem in front. We boys thought their hats ridiculous, but that didn't deter Kosciusko's heirs from clinging to their time-honored fashion. They absorbed the intense light of the Mediterranean sky, reddened, and shucked their skins like snakes. Gobbling up oranges, they walked the streets of Tel Aviv talking a soft, musical language and kissed the hands of women in a way that was even more outlandish than the style of their hats. They also funded a resurgence of prostitution in the Land of Israel.

Yes, of course we already had Jewish prostitutes. Also thieves. We had no need to hanker after them in our society, like the founding fathers of the Yishuv[1], in order to prove the complete normalization of the Jewish population in Palestine. And the Poles were, first and foremost, men. I can't say how the pickpockets fared, but the prostitutes positively flourished. The country had been flooded with soldiers even before the Polish additions, but during those months many of the other troops were rushed to Egypt to face the German offensive threatening Egypt and the rest of the Middle East. The Poles filled in the gaps.

On the day that is the backdrop to my story, I glided down the golden dunes of Tel Aviv to its beach. It was afternoon, late summer or early autumn. The lilies of Sharon were in bloom. Along the shore, bare feet left deep imprints in the coarse sand. The sun's rays stood out like coppery sheaves above the endless sea. Tidepools shimmered with tiny, dizzy fish. The rocks were smooth and slick with algae where the sea spray reached; beyond that point algae were dry and crumbly, and the rocks radiated the day's heat.

A little further up the beach, where your feet would sink into fine white sand and get scorched unless you stepped very quickly, a faded and threadbare rug was spread. On that rug, cleaving to each other as if they were one body, a Pole and a prostitute lay. Around them, passersby had gathered, their eyes squinted as if straining at a distant view. And around this whole scene, children were running in circles.

The soldier's cap was tossed on the sand, as if the man had ripped it off when he couldn't contain himself any longer. The back of his soldier's shirt was drenched with sweat. Drops of sweat glittered on his shaved nape, which was covered with fine fair hairs that had survived the razor; the hairs and droplets stood out in pale relief against the boiled red skin of his neck. The man's right arm was stretched along the edge of the rug, and his moist fingers kept opening and closing, as if he were being tortured. White grains of sand and beads of sweat dotted the burned skin of his hand.

How curious it is what memory still holds after so many years.

Later I heard people saying that the soldier and the woman had had an unseemly accident. Because of a sudden fright—no one seemed to know what—while having sex, the two "cleaved" to each other. More clinically, the muscles of the prostitute's vulva contracted around the Pole's penis and refused to relax. We kids had heard such stories,

---

[1] The Jewish population in Palestine.

particularly from the older boys whose sexual imaginations were heating up. The stories were terrifying, exciting, and horrible, but marvelous to listen to, marvelous to go over and over in one's thoughts when alone.

I joined the crowd, scared and attracted at the same time. Everyone's face bore an expression of supreme concentration, almost scholarly intensity. No one spoke and no one smiled. The sun beat pitilessly down on us, but no one moved. We stood there like sweating statues. A few of us breathed heavily, but no other noise interrupted the rustle of small waves breaking on the beach.

It is curious also what memory no longer holds: I can't say with certainty what happened next. But there is one thing I remember distinctly. I remember that woman's face. The soldier was trying to hide his face, tucked like a baby's into her armpit. She did nothing to cover hers. Only her eyes were closed, possibly from the sun's glare. Her dark brown face was simultaneously old and young, and her messy, bottle-blonde hair hung over it raggedly. The face expressed a deep, desperate shame, but also a sort of challenge, as if saying voicelessly: I'm better dead, but accept me as I am.

Her slack, almost lifeless mouth kept muttering, with a Sephardic accent, "Kids, go away . . . It's not nice, kids . . ."

That horrible, human shame, more than the challenge of someone with nothing to lose, burned into my memory. I doubt I truly understood what a prostitute was, and I was no expert on the mysteries of sex. Still, for very personal reasons I was sensitive to this human shame. God was my witness that I wanted to obey the pitiful pleading that fell incessantly from her slack lips. I just couldn't. My feet were annealed to the sand and refused to move.

Nausea filled me, and unbearable curiosity, and an overwhelming desire to run mixed with a leaden immobility that spread like a dark magic through my body's cells.

An ambulance came. Did someone call the Hadassa Municipal Hospital? It screeched to a halt on the road above the beach. Two paramedics dressed in white skidded down the sand hill with a stretcher. Right behind them, representing the forces of law and order, came a policeman in leather-belted khaki shorts. The paramedics grappled for a hold on the couple and lifted them onto the stretcher, immediately covering them with a blanket. The policeman, notebook in one hand and pencil in the other, scribbled vaguely in his notebook while yelling at the crowd. "Kids go home! Go home!" he shouted, face flushed and angry. To the adults he added, "and you, aren't you ashamed? What is this, a movie?"

A sort of moan drifted out of the crowd, like the twang of a suddenly loosened wire. People obeyed the policeman, first as a matter of principle (a Jewish policeman, one of *ours*), and secondly, maybe, from a belated sense of guilt.

Once on the stretcher, the prostitute opened her eyes: dark, tired eyes, filled with unshed tears that could have risen either from grief and shame or from the painful dazzle of the sun. Did her eyes meet mine, or am I imagining that from the distance of so many years? She muttered something I couldn't make out, groaned, and turned her eyes away.

The paramedics rushed awkwardly up the sand hill. Sweat darkened their white uniforms and made patterns under their armpits. The ambulance door opened to admit the stretcher and one paramedic; the other took the wheel. The engine grudgingly came to life; the ambulance coughed a curl of blue smoke, heaved in reverse, and then moved forward. The driver turned onto Keren Kayemet Boulevard, picked up speed, and went out of sight. He didn't sound the siren.

We kept thrashing out the incident over and over. Our imaginations ran like wildfire. It was terrifying and fascinating. Later on, the fear of "cleaving" became inseparable from our erotic fantasies, like an invisible axe hanging overhead.

For a long time I went on seeing the whore's eyes. Dark, extinguished, but alive enough to plead. They faded only gradually.

After all, consciousness retains only what it can hold. It is a process of inevitable sifting which enables us to survive. We experience something we think we'll never forget, but we do. Even the most appalling scenes, ones that happen before our very own wondering and stricken eyes, get pushed aside by other, more private humiliations.

And did it really happen as I've told it? Did the prostitute and the Polish soldier truly "cleave" to each other in the flesh with a horrible intimacy that couldn't be ended until—so the story went—the doctor on duty gave them a shot that made their muscles relax and expand?

I don't know.

I do know that the Poles left the country and went to Egypt. Later they arrived on the battlefields of Italy, and many of them were buried in its soil. Only a few returned to their homeland. Where did the soldier from the Tel Aviv beach wander to? I can never have an answer to this question. And the prostitute—she probably went on practicing her trade, the oldest of all human occupations, as long as her muscles went on serving her.

Translated by Laura Fargas

Staffs

My face was slashed open twice. The first time with staffs during a training session under the auspices of my underground, the Hagana.[1] The second, after we cleared the walls recently plastered with broadsheets by the I.Z.L.[2] The first time blood was drawn by a friend, the second time by an enemy. The blows were almost identical and just about in the same part of my face. Clearly, I handled the staff very poorly. I never learned to protect myself in training and always adhered to the best and worst of my athletic tradition. And when the squad that accompanied the broadside operation used their staffs against us, it was impossible for me to escape unharmed. I was too clumsy to evade the blows.

From the very beginning, my high school instructor gave up on me. Being Hungarian, with a good sense of humor, he understood that I was a lost cause. He did his best to improve my muscular equipment without exerting himself. My instructors in the youth brigade of the Hagana were tougher. I tried with mind, body, and soul. It was in vain. I was a classic intellectual—all brain, no brawn. Therefore, because of my relative youth—I was younger than most of my classmates—I had

---

[1]The primary Jewish underground organization in British mandated Palestine, which took orders from the democratically elected National Executive of the Yishuv, a mass organization which later became the basis of the Israeli army.

[2]The Irgun Zevai Leumi (National Military Organization). Seceding from the Hagana in the early 1930s, the I.Z.L. became the armed underground of the Jewish right, preaching active defiance of the British authorities and consistent resistance and retaliation *vis-à-vis* the Arabs.

to use the whole range of my intellectual potential to gain equal, if not superior, status. To survive the natural competition, which included impressing the girls in the brigade, I resorted to a dazzling display of wit, erudition, and even a taste for poetry. Although these virtues endowed me with a vaguely romantic character, I was, alas, still a loser in the world of the physique. Athletics, staff fighting, and field craft were impossible for me.

I left the pioneer youth movement when I reached the top level in my high school. The school was a bastion of Zionist socialist youth movements. The main goal was to encourage students either to found a new kibbutz or to adhere to one already established. The paramount objectives were to settle the land (thus contributing to the historic task of rebuilding the ancient heritage of the Jewish people), and to hold the ground against British rulers and Arab antagonists. In fact, I was still in elementary school when I joined the pioneer youth movement— the movement closest to my parents' political and social beliefs.

In that youth organization, affiliated with a kibbutz movement, I belonged to a "naval cell." Boys and girls huddled together in a decrepit shack located in the heart of the dunes, far to the north of Tel Aviv. Our closest neighbor was a well-known teachers' seminary. Innocents that we were, we dreamed of founding a kibbutz of fishermen and farmers. Therefore, our instructors taught us a class on "sea-going." This mainly consisted of the art of tying sailors' knots. At times, they fired up our imaginations with tales of storms at sea, courageous mariners, and sailing on the high seas. But most of the time we spent tying knots and learning how to row a boat on the Yarkon River.

The knots I tied had very little shape. True to form, my hands twisted the rope in every direction but the right one. Totally unacceptable to my teachers! As for the boat, there was always a struggle with rebellious oars. Like a slave in a Roman galley, I sprayed great torrents of water all around me. It was hopeless. My sole pleasure lay in the tales of courage and derring-do. Sometimes I would pick up the threads of the narrative and embroider imaginative, action-packed sequels.

My vocabulary grew out of both original and translated works. I memorized whole paragraphs from my favorite books which included *Without a Star* by Yehuda Burla;[3] a Hebrew translation of Dickens'

---

[3]Yehuda Burla (1886-1964) was born in Jerusalem of an old Sephardic family. He wrote exotic stories about Arabs and Bedouins.

The Pickwick Papers; Sholem Aleichem, translated by his son-in-law, Y. D. Berkowitz; and the great historical novels of the Polish author, Henryk Sienkiewiez, superbly translated into Hebrew.[4]

This passion for linguistics and vocabulary created a wall between my friends and myself. Why didn't I talk like ordinary people? Was I mocking them? Did I think myself too good for them? At times, my friends were unable to understand me. They were baffled by idioms and stilted phrases straight out of my favorite books. Quoting from Sienkiewiez' *Fire and Sword* or *Flood*, I would greet them with: "Your most humble servant, Sir Knight." This did not go over well and my friends were quick to retaliate. I soon learned my lesson and dropped the offending flowers of speech from my vocabulary.

But my rebuffs did not discourage me from reading. From the wars between the Poles and the Cossacks I went on to devour the best of world literature in Hebrew translation published under the renowned Stiebel imprint in my own country and abroad. But as I continued reading, the space between my two selves grew wider. My despairing parents struggled to keep alive my interest in the "movement." They even turned for help to my high school principal, Dr. Tony Halle. She was famous among the students for her intimate talks, because Tony tried to find a common ground between us. In her thick German accent, she explained all the good things—personal, public, ideological—about the pioneer youth movements. Then she elaborated on the dangers of exaggerated individualism. I did not argue with her, because I knew that she was right.

The problem was my position in a defined reality. I could agree with the right of the pioneer youth movement to exist and flourish, just as I could agree with the obstacles presented by exaggerated individu-

---

[4]Henryk Sienkiewiez (1846-1916) was one of Poland's greatest novelists, the author of *Quo Vadis* and Nobel Prize winner. He was also the author of a trilogy about 17th century Poland. The Hebrew translation of his first volume, *Fire and Sword* (1919), ignited a fiery polemic between Y. Ch. Brenner (1880-1921), Hebrew writer and critic, and Zeev (Vladimir) Jabotinsky (1880-1940), writer and founding leader of the rightist nationalist Revisionist Party, which served as a political umbrella to the I.Z.L. Brenner condemned "the novel of the petite Polish nobility" as hollow in spirit and overflowing with bloodshed. Jabotinsky defended it as a literary work, boosting the morale of young readers by its descriptions of brave exploits and intense action.

alism. But I found it impossible to remain a part of the organic collective. Nothing could stop the division, the drifting away, not even the pleasure of sharing guard duty with a girl in a miserable shack from night until morning. I could tolerate ideological clashes, personal differences. But rampant individualism was my undoing. I was unable to resist the onslaught.

Perhaps the problem of position and reality began early in my childhood, in Tel Aviv. When I was still young, I would escape to the beach whenever I felt lonely or discouraged. In the summer I would head toward the moist *zifzif*[5] at the sea's edge, the golden sandy slope scorching my feet. What dreams I had in the shelter of the cliffs, towering above the beach! I was intoxicated by the smells of iodine and salt, enchanted by the green lights of little waves flowing gently in and out of my hiding place. It was a long and difficult step from my private sea world to the youth movement. Family pressures and the moral dictates of public opinion forced me to join. Secretly, I knew I had no place among the kibbutz enthusiasts, the seafarers, or the tillers of the soil. Books were my true passion. That passion, or obsession, became so intense that my parents were terrified. I was reading and writing simultaneously, far beyond the first phase of passive absorption. It was this passion which produced my break with the youth movement. I dropped out because of the unavoidable clash between a stubborn individual and a demanding collective.

The rupture with the youth movement did not affect my relationship with the Youth Brigade of the Hagana. Never did I renounce or go back on my oath to the Hagana, sworn on a revolver in a dark room as my heart pounded with excitement. On my bicycle, I carried secret messages to important Hagana officials, under the very nose of British officialdom. I ran, jumped, even waved a staff in face-to-face training battles. I learned, in a limited way, how to use small fire arms. I was completely dedicated, in spite of my physical deficiencies.

In the historic summer of 1948, my older classmates were drafted into the burgeoning Israeli army. I was too young to go with them, and, to my shame, was forced to stay at home with the girls and younger children. But in June of that year, I suddenly discovered that even incorrigible individuals like myself could be useful. One shining summer day I was taken to Hayarkon Street in Tel Aviv, along with other

---

[5]Gravel or coarse sand.

members of the flotsam and jetsam bunch. There, on the road which ran parallel to the beach, we were ordered to prevent all unauthorized people from going down to the water line. Not far from shore, the *Altalena* (the I.Z.L. arms ship), floated peacefully in the quiet water. Ben Gurion, head of the government, claimed that the ship was a spearhead of an insurrection planned by the I.Z.L.

The I.Z.L. vehemently denied this. The government ordered the ship to surrender. The *Altalena's* crew and passengers refused. The government then ordered the army to destroy the ship. Armed Palmach soldiers[6] took positions along the promenade. The Red House, a former Hagana headquarters, was bursting with activity. The shooting began. Thuds from the single artillery piece—the army could not spare another gun—drowned out the rifle cracks. Flames rose from the ship. The reserves, to which I belonged, had no fire arms. Even if the army had enough to pass around, I doubt if we would have known how to use them. Instead of fire arms, we were given staffs. Straight, handsome, sturdy staffs, something we were familiar with, something we understood. Within each of us, the eager, immature youth merged with the man. The circle was complete.

Translated by Cicely Angleton

---

[6]The Palmach were crack units of the Hagana and later of the Israeli army during the War of Liberation.

First Publication

Her face is not clear in my memory. It floats in a haze that obscures the shape of her nose, her chin, the cut of her eyes, the feel of her skin. Perhaps her features are not distinctive enough for me to recall. But I'm certain she had a pretty face—full but firm, with a captivating, mischievous smile. And, as I write this, the haze lifts a bit, so that now I remember she had blue eyes. But I don't recall the color of her hair. Mostly what I remember is the way she walked, with her arms slightly frozen at her side. It was as if her arms defied the rhythm of her body, keeping to a slower, independent motion of their own. I liked that motion very much, though I could not then—or now—explain why.

I was either a junior or a senior in high school. She was about the same age, but she didn't go to my school. I don't recall how we met. But I know that I almost immediately fell in love with her, her blue eyes, her ample bust, that icy walk. Certain she had suitors to spare, I began courting her in my earnest but clumsy way. I showered her with a torrent of literary talk, trying to impress her with my intellectual prowess. Alas, she was no intellectual. Poetry didn't appeal to her. But she was no fool, and her ambivalence to poetry didn't make her less attractive to me. On the contrary. And she knew how to listen gracefully.

It seems to me now that I should have let my fingers speak to her instead, in that language that transcends words. Hers was a ripening body, resonant with vibrations, begging to be fondled, to be aroused. But I was overwhelmed by doubts and anxieties. All my daring seduction plans evaporated each time we went strolling on clear summer evenings along the boulevard that now bears Ben Gurion's name. Even when we settled among the tamarisks, on a bench half sunk in shadows—a place so suited to intimacy—even then, with my heart pounding insanely and my eyes dim with desire and fear, I didn't cross the line. At most, I fluttered my parched lips, as if by accident, over her hair, or gave her bare, full arms an occasional, seemingly random stroke. Possibly I offered her a brief, burning kiss that flickered into nowhere. But my fears were too real, my fantasies too daring. Later, I read that Tolstoy, who certainly seemed to be an authority on the subject of women, claimed that even a girl of fifteen desires a man to take her. But I didn't know that then.

I did write a few passionate poems about her. But they were unripe, immature, and would probably have faded away without a trace had not my father, in some mysterious way, discovered one of them. Mysterious, that is, because I never let my father even so much as glance at my "literary work." Even then, at the very beginning, an opaque partition separated us in all matters pertaining to my artistic experiments. As the years went by and I became more deeply involved in writing, that barrier between father and son rose in height until it towered between us.

But back then, my father was curious about my scribbling. He was, at best, an infrequent and shallow reader of poetry; however, I'm sure he shuffled through my papers when I was out of the house. There was really no way to hide anything in our small house, cramped beyond endurance because of the lodgers we had to take in. So it wouldn't have been difficult for my father to discover my love poems. He took one of them—probably the one he liked best—to Gabriel Talpir, a poet and art critic who had founded the magazine *Gazit*. Took one, that is, without saying a word to me.

Talpir took pity on that first fruit of my poetic orchard. Rather than throw it away, he accepted it for publication. My father kept silent. How long the poem awaited its turn to be published, I don't know; *Gazit* didn't keep to a regular schedule. It was printed whenever the devoted editor raised enough money to finance the next issue. And when *Gazit* finally appeared with my poem included, my father triumphantly brought a copy home and laid it on the kitchen table.

There was my poem. It was mine, mine only, from beginning to end, brimming with adolescent ardor.

In a classic Sholem Aleichem story, the protagonist, one Shmuel Shmelkis, craves to be a writer. When finally something by his pen is published in a magazine, he rushes into the streets of the *shtetl* waving the magazine and bellowing, "I'm published! I'm published!" But the passersby misunderstand him; they think he is shouting "I'm punished! I'm punished!"—that he has been arrested by the police for some revolutionary or criminal act. Aleichem's story flitted across my mind even as a storm of feelings flooded every cell of my body. That poem, printed under my own unmistakable name, invited every reader into my secret world of anguished love. My innermost thoughts, exposed for all the world to see. Blood pounding in my face, my ears ringing, I got up and rushed out of the kitchen, out of the house.

Later I returned, terribly enraged, demanding an apology from my father. How dare he take a private manuscript, without my knowledge, and use it as if it were his own? I fired poisonous accusations at him; he shot back with harsh, bitter words. Certainly he had been driven by good intentions, but I was repulsed by what I deemed a gross invasion of my privacy, a transgression that was unforgivable.

Deeply hurt, I threw the magazine away, as though it were something abominable. Only later, when no one was around, did I retrieve the magazine and read the poem. Only then did I feel a warm wave of pleasure surging through me. The love I had failed to consummate on the bench in the boulevard, amid the salt-scented tamarisk trees, bloomed redolent and real, real as the black ink glistening on the smooth white page.

Looking back, I can see that the poem had no literary value. But that's beside the point. More to the point is that shudder, that singular shiver that fledgling poets feel coursing through their veins on seeing their first poem in print. It's a momentary compensation for the failure of desire, enabling them to behold distant shores, almost close enough to touch.

I didn't tell anyone about the poem or its publication, not even my closest friends. But one morning, my literature teacher dug a copy of *Gazit* out of his briefcase and asked the class to listen. A hush spread over the room as he slowly and dramatically read my poem aloud. When he finished, he added a few kind and warm-hearted words of his own addressed to the still unnamed poet. Only then did he divulge the author's identity to the audience, who sat in stunned silence, looking at me. If only the ground could have opened up and swallowed me!

Then, a blessing: the bell rang, and my classmates got up to leave. Some of them came over and slapped me on the back. Others simply smiled. But I was drowning in a sea of shame and only wanted the day to be over, so that I could slink away and hide until the whole affair was forgotten.

It was forgotten, of course, by them if not by me. But one thing I remember distinctly: that blue-eyed, big-bosomed girl showed no more interest in me than before; her arms remained frozen at her sides. So it was I who thawed instead, freed of that strange spell she had cast on me. Why did the attraction fade? Why does it ever? Why did it erupt in the first place? It's all part of that complex, painful, sometimes ridiculous process we call growing up. If we ever do.

Translated by Marilyn Millstone

Star Particles

In May 1947, while yet a boy, I took an oath of allegiance to the Hagana. My voice quavering in the dark, my hand resting on a pistol, I repeated the words clearly after the commander. A year later, on the day the state of Israel was declared, I was busy as an official member of the Hagana Youth Brigade digging trenches on the Dov airstrip north of Tel Aviv.

When the Egyptian planes arrived, we fell down on our bellies, behind the cactus hedges or in half-dug trenches. I remember the rattle of machine guns, the thuds of bombs hurled from low-flying aircraft, and columns of dust raised by bullets hitting the ground. My lips were dry, my heart pounded—of course, by any standard of air raids, it was ridiculous.

The War of Liberation was on, and our new nation, under attack by seven Arab armies, needed soldiers. Within days my 17-year-old schoolmates had been taken into the army. Left behind were only girls and the younger boys. Burning with shame because I was too young, I tried in desperation to hoodwink an enlistment officer, who was only amused. Later I looked for contacts to ease my way into a uniform, to no avail.

In June the *Altalena* arrived. Grasping staffs, the younger boys stood along certain streets leading to the beach. Our official goal was to keep order, acting as a graceful addition to the armed Palmach troops. That was a fiery Israeli summer, with a green sea glittering in the sun, and a smell of burning and smoke.

It was the first chapter in the scroll of independence. A short time later we learned who had died among our schoolmates. The names of the dead came like lightning bolts, striking an air suddenly emptied of its essence. How could we go on studying? Formally we had to attend our regular classes, except on those occasions when we were needed. But our teachers understood that school was impossible.

We wandered along Hayarkon Street to chat with the colorful human mass, speaking many languages, crowding its confines. Among them were English-speaking volunteers; survivors of the Holocaust, communicating in Yiddish; and young Jews from North Africa, chatting in French to whomever would listen. The fledgling air force headquarters was just down the street; the men who entered or left it were crowned with glory in our eyes. There were also prostitutes, an inevitable accompaniment to any concentration of troops—women who filled the mind with strange thoughts, utterly contradicting the tenets of the youth movement and the underground.

Things happened so quickly that time seemed to rush by like an express train. Or perhaps I imagine that now, while back then it crawled like a turtle in plate armor. As the months passed, my soldier friends returned, proud of their military exploits, and rejoined our class so that they could graduate. As the war ended, Israel began absorbing multitudes of new immigrants from all over the world. With that came different pains and joys, not the unique, exceptionally powerful anguish and exultation that marked the war.

Then began my first serious literary struggles with all their cravings and disappointments. University life was both bohemian and innocent as I tried to imitate the "cursed poets" of French modernism. Alcohol, love, jealousy, hope—now they are mere words, letters, syllables, devoid of the tension of life after so long a time. Dust of years called "memories." Fatigue.

And yet, a miracle begins. Resurrection, moving from the collective to the personal. The breast inhales and exhales. The face flushes, a spark is rekindled in the eyes. The redemption of small delights. No longer conquering the world, only a passionate seizing of a fragment. No more pretensions. I recall the lines by Ya'akov Steinberg:

> I will settle under the cover of smoke, a lighted cigarette in
>   my mouth,
> its hue like that of consolation, so smoky and grim.
> Smoke in consolation's eye, not seeing anything anymore.
> I'll sit here until the door stops turning on its hinge.
> Deceiving fate, like a clown, spread idle words,
> and channels of prattle run dry and then are renewed;

Here is also only a passage of lie traversed by people,
also all global passages trembling over nothingness.
Facing futilely-lusting women my desires are yet unconsumed
and in the midst of multitudes, I'll respond to my soul.
But who will tell me: there's something better—go there?
Darkness fills life's shed. And in a hidden trough of night
all the sweet and bitter berries of our life.

At the halfway point of my life, I discover how intimately I feel about poems that previously left me indifferent; my soul reflects the body's biological change. Why do I remember so vividly the smell of dry earth at the Dov airstrip so many years ago? The faded green and yellow hues of prickly cactus plants? Sweat dripping from my brow, calluses blossoming on my palms after days of digging, the hammering of blood in my temples?

Why do I still recall the brilliant green of the summer sea and the smoke pinching my nostrils? My memory is stamped with a sinful craving, in the very fibers of my flesh, for a Moroccan girl in a tight-fitting dress, eyes painted, breasts thrust forward, who hung on the arm of a young soldier. And I recall the shame of being left behind.

I cling to the tiny particulars of the tangible past. An expanse of golden sand lighted by a lonely electric pole. The sweet clicking of a water pump in the thick of an orchard. The cool touch of a tiled floor while the *khamsin* hammers with burning fists on closed shutters. Green tiles with black beauty stripes. The scent of jasmine suddenly flooding an alley. A tiny, incognizant movement of a girl's hand that charms my heart. A sultry night of guarding the youth movement's shack, when a boy discovers, at about midnight, that he is a man, and the girl becomes aware of her budding womanliness.

I return, and then move on . . . a worn, pulverized body, bombarded by star particles, a shower from outer space. Terrified of darkness, stretching hands to the flickering past.

The motherland is not a name, an ideology, a naked thought. It appears in a mosaic of small, living, tangible images. The Land of Israel—it glows in my blood, flesh, and nerves. The motherland is the country in my soul, whether asleep or awake, and in all the dark and shining labyrinths of time.

Translated by Eva Greene

The Mistake

In the beginning was the error.

When I went up to the university in Jerusalem I was merely a boy. Not even seventeen. This chronological fact has nothing to do with the shape of my landscape, "My Land of Israel," of memory and desire, without which I would not have become what I am. By the winter closing the year 1949 I had already stored in myself all the basic components needed to sustain my "ulterior soul." In a very concentrated way—because of the unique quality of time in our area as well as my particular characteristics—I had absorbed and conserved the basic elements necessary to the development of a concrete artist. (I don't believe in abstract artists.) Colors, smells, sounds: I already had taken them in on principle. Only the superstructure was lacking. This I constructed with endless anguish during the years allotted me on a scaffolding of experience and experiments, expectations and disappointments, joys and sorrows.

Well, on being swept into the whirlpool of student life, I was almost immediately mistaken for somebody else. A sensitive boy, burgeoning poet, plucked out of his birthplace in the coastal plain and hurled into a mountainous existence, I would have that winter etched in my memory by the cruelty of its cold. The immense thirst for life bubbling in my veins struggled with my timidity. This, of course, was no news. Since early childhood I had carved a space for myself among my elders. And yet the present struggle was more complex. Most of the students were veterans—it was the first year after the War of Liberation—and war-scarred maturity was a basic ingredient of the new reality. Anyway, the mistake was committed almost immediately when I climbed the stairs of "Terra Sancta," the monastery requisitioned for the faculty of humanities of the Hebrew University in Jerusalem.

Out of a noisy group which swarmed around the main entry to the building shot the voice of a round-faced fellow—curiously enough, the roundness was the only feature that struck me. Very brief he was, straight to the point:

"You! You!"

I looked at him. He was absolutely unknown to me. I prepared to march on.

He didn't stop. "One moment! One moment!"

And bursting out of the group, he caught me by the arm, obviously happy to discover me.

"So you too have managed to arrive here?"

And without giving me time to consider his query, he lowered his voice instinctively and said:

"I don't know your name, but I recognize your face . . . You were a member of the L.H.Y.[1] youth, weren't you?"

I gaped in amazement.

"What the hell?"

He laughed.

"I've been endowed with excellent perceptiveness. Once I see somebody, I never forget the face. Like a camera. I saw you once, pasting broadsheets. I was in Security."

And still talking with a low voice, he added:

"Don't be afraid. Now it's okay to talk."

I tried to point out his mistake. I had never been in the L.H.Y. Not even the L.H.Y. Youth. On the contrary, I had belonged to the Hagana.

He refused to listen:

"For heaven's sake . . . What are you afraid of? That's not a shame. And I'm not wrong. Perceptiveness, you know."

How can one argue with perceptiveness?

Even after I told him my name, he refused to give up. While introducing me to his friends, most of whom had naturally been active

---

[1]The Lohamei Herut Yisrael, or Fighters for the Freedom of Israel, the most extreme Jewish underground group in pre-independence Palestine. Seceding from the I.Z.L. in 1940, the L.H.Y. represented individual terror and uncompromising struggle against the British (who nicknamed the group "the Stern Gang"). Among its leaders was Yitzhak Shamir, who was later to become Prime Minister of Israel.

in the ranks of the "dissidents,"[2] he insisted on revealing what he believed to be my hidden past.

There was no use relying on my name as proof of non-involvement; in the underground, people were known by their *noms de guerre*, not their real names.

What happened later to the round-faced fellow? I don't know. But one thing I do know: whenever we ran into each other on the academic trail, he would mention my supposed origins, good-naturedly reproaching me for a lack of pride in such a glorious chapter in my history.

Deep in my secret heart I *was* proud of that mistake. Even considering the oath of allegiance I had sworn to the Hagana, it would be an exaggeration to assume I was anything more than an intellectual with two left hands and an over-active imagination. My courage, if it existed, was definitely more spiritual than physical. But I did have fantasies and was jealous of those intrepid armed fighters, children of deep darkness. Indeed, toward the end of my high school days, whenever I was beset by a desire "to do something," I would think of the L.H.Y. as though it were enveloped by some magical haze, the brains of its martyrs strewn like white roses[3] over remote paths.

I didn't cross the lines. I wasn't *that* rash.

Why do I tell all this?

Because my mistaken identity enhanced my reputation in the eyes of a lanky fellow who was also standing at the top of the stairs among the former "dissidents." A jacket was nonchalantly but deliberately thrown over his shoulders. When he was excited or angry his blue eyes became steely. The carelessness of the jacket and the steely hue of the eyes immediately appealed to me.

The tall guy studied law, but the wide range of his knowledge struck me dumb. He would immerse himself in literature and philosophy, quoting extensively from the books he'd read. He was particularly

---

[2]A derogatory nickname referring to the I.Z.L. and L.H.Y. undergrounds, mostly used in Hagana circles.

[3]An allusion to a poem by Ya'ir (Abraham Stern), a scholar, poet, and founder of the L.H.Y., killed by the British in 1942.

fond of Uri Zvi Greenberg's[4] poetry and considered him the most important contemporary Hebrew poet.

We became friends. He treated me like a younger brother, excusing my faults patiently and sympathetically as the inevitable result of my youth and lack of self-confidence, which I sometimes disguised with a veneer of arrogance. I guess he defended me also because of my supposed membership in the L.H.Y. Youth—a beacon in the dark night of my stupidity.

Probably more for his authoritative air than for his erudition, I nicknamed him Jupiter. (To me, the Roman Jupiter sounded better than the Greek Zeus.) I owe my introduction to the poetry of Uri Zvi Greenberg to Jupiter.

Of course I had heard of Uri Zvi Greenberg before I met Jupiter, but his poems had no foothold either at home or at school. The few poems that had crept into my possession were usually tainted by hatred.

Jupiter—that nickname rapidly became popular, particularly among the young writers who later laid the foundation for the Likrat group[5]— was the first to open a window through which I could view the wide spaces of Uri Zvi Greenberg's poetry.

Fortunately, Jupiter had a keen aesthetic sense. He wasn't satisfied with only the polemic or rightist-nationalist aspects of Greenberg's writing, which certainly corresponded to his own opinions, but equally enjoyed the poet's lyrical gifts. Indeed, the first collection of Greenberg's poems that I held in my hands was *Anacreon on the Pole of Sadness*. This, the original edition under a tattered black cover, was given to me by Jupiter. When he discovered how much I liked Greenberg's lyrical poetry, Jupiter just let me keep the book. I think I still have it in my possession, only the cover has fallen off and vanished.

We used to sit at Café Hermon in Rehavia.[6] I dropped in there at every opportunity in that uneasy period when my spiritual and material

---

[4]Uri Zvi Greenberg (1896-1981), a great Hebrew poet, was well known for his fervent nationalistic verse and was the author of *Anacreon on the Pole of Sadness*.

[5]The Likrat, or "Toward" group, consisted of young writers who in the early 1950s instigated a modernist revolution in Israeli Hebrew *belles lettres*.

[6]A quarter in western Jerusalem.

distresses commingled. There, under the casuarina trees, sipping a chilly glass of tea, Jupiter lectured on the merits of Greenberg's poetry which, since then, has always reminded me of the flickering lights and shades of coniferous trees. It seems to me that in judging the phenomenon of Likrat by his severe ideological and aesthetic criteria, Jupiter regretted its conception. The anti-political Likrat was not what he expected of young poets. In any case, he went on loaning me poetry books and, even if he inevitably began to suspect the truth of my past, he kept being my friend. I remember he even gave me Pinchas Sadeh's[7] first book of poems, *Massa Dumah* [Tribute to the dead], shrewdly tracing its sources of inspiration.

I learned quite a lot from Jupiter about masters and disciples as well as influences, conscious and unconscious. His sharp verdict, sometimes merciless, was not, I think now, always just, but in giving it he was honest.

The Anacreonic sadness of Uri Zvi Greenberg fascinated me:

And in the light of the covenant arrived that moment:
And the golden crown, too, weighs the Emperor down, heavy
    as the cliff.
And the Emperor is a body: *sad in the blood and tired.*
And on the bottom of the Pole he is standing barefooted.
And royalty rolls off the heart like a stone . . .

The Anacreon verses were, for me, an intoxicating discovery. That clear and private grief flowed through my being and bubbled like an alcoholic high. How did that stubborn individualism—"And I prefer to be an aching body / for the sake of the nail of my pink finger / which is so cute"—merge with the nationalist mysticism, staggering under the burden of the people's destiny? Even Jupiter couldn't explain that. No, human beings were not going to sacrifice themselves on such an individualistic pole as if it were an historical altar.

This is a wholly different sacrifice. But it conformed to the absolutely private pains and doubts which tormented me then. Jerusalem was torn apart, slashed by barbed-wire fences, anti-tank barriers, and defense trenches. Where I lived, a dormitory previously serving as the

---

[7]Pinchas Sadeh (1929-1994) is an Israeli Hebrew poet and novelist, influenced early in his writing career by Uri Zvi Greenberg.

headquarters of the Christian Society for the Distribution of the Holy Books faced the positions of the Arab Legion, as the Jordanian army was then called. Bullets would whistle over the roof. But the tear which ripped my flesh and soul was as tangible as that rending the city, if not more. The symbolic significance is born at a later stage, when youth is not so exposed to the direct touch of life.

Jupiter, in any case, did not adopt such an attitude. People like Jupiter protect themselves with walls whose stones, like Jerusalem's stones, are hewn from the ribs of mountains. On the peaks of these mountains, prophets speak face to face with their gods. I suspected that Jupiter was not only a diligent reader but also a secret writer of—poetry? fiction? meditations? He neither denied nor admitted, but simply cloaked himself with silence, his eyes becoming steely. Many years went by, years when he worked as a government attorney, before he displayed even a hint. Then, suddenly he came out with both fiction and poetry. His views—so it seems from my present observation post— didn't change. They just became more extreme, perhaps more desperate.

All those years we didn't see each other. I guess that finally he concluded that I hadn't been a member of the L.H.Y. Youth after all, not even as a paster of broadsheets.

But I still read the Anacreon poems in the same tattered book, whose pages have already yellowed. Emperors, ministers, commoners— all of them, sad-in-blood and tired, stand barefoot on the bottom of the Pole.

Translated by Elaine Magarrell

Poets to Come:
Roots of Likrat

Writing a memoir is no fun. Sometimes it's even frightening.

There is the fear of passing time, of added years, and of that double-helixed hourglass whose sand mercilessly grows less . . .

Moreover, there is no promise of objectivity in the writing of memoirs. Memory plays tricks with the mind, and one's inclinations about what or who to write about, and what to say, have a hand in the matter. I therefore do not pretend to objectivity. It is no consolation that certain chapters of these reminiscences are flimsy, some the innocent victims of chronology, and others subject to my own disappointments. All, regrettably, are impaired. However, and this is not an apology but an assertion of fact, almost four decades have passed since the first seeds were sown by that group of writers now known as "The Generation of the State." What is recorded here has been filtered by the lengthening backward-flowing rivers of time.

In the beginning was the University.

I refer to the Hebrew University in Jerusalem and the first academic year after the War of Liberation (1949-1950), an irrelevant fact because the people with whom I would struggle to publish a literary magazine called *Likrat* I didn't meet until the following year. Most of them, however, had committed themselves to studying literature that year. My studies, not unrelated but along significantly different lines, were in modern history and political science.

Why, then, did we meet?

We met because it couldn't have been otherwise. Our Jerusalem was small in those years. The Faculty of Humanities was installed in the "Terra Sancta" building, and the Faculty of Law, in another monastery—"Ratisbone," near the Bezalel Art Academy. In the second year of my Jerusalem life, I moved to the student's dormitory at the

Bible House on the partition between Israeli and Jordanian territories (the roof was out of bounds because the Jordanian army fielded snipers); despite the fact that male and female students lived in separate quarters, the dormitory bustled with busy and merry life. The air, inside and out, so it seems to me today, was scented all year with the fragrance of the surrounding pines.

Two other students and I shared a huge room in the dormitory. One of them later became a physics professor; the other, a cynical parliamentary correspondent. Both probably remember the crazy poet who kept unholy hours, sometimes returning at the crack of dawn to insist on writing down what the muses had dictated to his feverish mind.

The madness that was writing had, of course, existed in me before my arrival at the university. All of us, the Likrat people, had been at it—some secretly, some openly—before becoming acquainted with one another. But during the first year of my Jerusalem life, a certain tension was mounting in hidden channels, and those channels burst their banks and flowed together in the second year when we began meeting regularly and with purpose.

Even before I went to Jerusalem, I had published "poems." I use quotation marks here, and rightly so, for not one of us was a sixteen-year-old Rimbaud gone to shock poetical Paris. I had published my attempts in *Bama'aleh* [Up the hill], the bi-weekly magazine of the Working Youth Federation. It was edited by Moshe Mossenson, a member of Kibbutz Na'an and author of *Letters from the Desert*, an epistolary book describing his experiences in the Palestinian Jewish units of the British army then deployed in the western desert of North Africa.[1] Mossenson was a unique personality, endowed with an exceptionally kind and understanding heart and a magnificent sense of humor. He encouraged fledgling writers among the teen-aged proletariat as well as high school students and members of the various pioneer youth movements. My work also appeared in Gabriel Talpir's *Gazit*, still retaining at that time some of the *sturm-und-drang* of the avant-garde of the 1930s. Aryeh Sivan could have taken pride in the one poem, "Davar," he managed to publish in the *Supplement for Recruits*, the Federation of Labor's daily, whose literary editors were famous (or infamous) for their rigid conservative tastes. Sivan, born and raised in

---

[1]Present-day Libya.

Tel Aviv, also a former Palmach member, was a swarthy, fiery-eyed fellow who worked at Kibbutz Me'oz Chayim. Moshe Ben-Shaul, scion of an old Jerusalem family, also had been a Palmachnik. In those days, he was a member of Kibbutz Gevim in the Negev (he later became the editor of the magazine published for the youth of the Kibbutz movement). From the army also came Natan Zach, fair of skin and hair, who, in spite of arriving in the country when he was five, never lost his slight German accent. Zach, incidentally, studied literature and philosophy, and his first poem appeared in 1950 in the magazine published by the youth guard of the ruling Labor Party, a fact he was later keen to erase from his records because of his avowed anti-establishment views.

We met, finally, in the corridors of "Terra Sancta." And at Nitzan on Ben Yehuda Street, a café where the air was thick with cigarette smoke, and, in the winter, heated by stoves until the atmosphere was almost (but, of course, not quite) insufferable. And also under the casuarina trees of Hermon, a café on Rehavia, not far from the buildings of the Jewish Agency. But, mostly, we met in the attic-like space occupied by Binyamin Herushovsky.[2]

Binyamin—better known under his *nom de plume* H. Binyamin—also was fair-skinned with hair so blond it was almost white. He had a long Semitic nose and clever eyes. And he was older than the rest of us. After studying in a Hebrew Tarbut school[3] in Lithuania, he fled to the Soviet Union in the wake of the Nazi invasion, and I think he spent time at a Soviet university, possibly in Moscow, before arriving at a displaced persons camp in post-war Germany. He managed to publish two collections of Yiddish poetry while in Germany before emigrating to Israel, where he would fight in the War of Liberation and write his long-lined, spacious, expressionist poems. When I met him, he was living in a room on the roof of a tall building across from Frumin House where the Knesset had been installed before its present splendid abode was built. Nearby, on the same floor, lived Yossef Lichtenboim, who was gloomy, suspicious, and immersed in translating *Pan Tadeusz*, Adam Mickiewicz's great Polish epic. How many floors led to those

---

[2]Now known as Benjamin Harshav, a professor at Yale University.

[3]Tarbut, or Culture schools were a system of Hebrew schools established in pre-World War II Poland and Lithuania.

rooms? I don't remember, but we would take the staircase by storm, galloping up like young stallions.

Binyamin possessed an extraordinary memory, one capable of retaining every word he ever read, and his erudition both amazed and embarrassed us. He knew three languages—German, Russian, and, of course, Yiddish—and could recite by heart complete excerpts from the manifestoes of the modernist movements. Although Zach also had mastered German and was fluent in English and French, we considered Binyamin the final authority on the history of literature.

And so Binyamin would sit in his small room, at the desk loaded down with books and copybooks, and, with marvelous concentration, study, at times through the commotion of spirited arguments about what we felt was the very essence of the creative process. When he interjected, he did so gently, patiently, and with an ironic, sober light in his eyes. There were also times, late at night when I was royally drunk, that I would go to see Binyamin. With his limitless patience, he would prepare coffee to sober me up before returning to his studies. I don't remember his ever losing self-control, not even once.

Binyamin's coffee was probably one of the greatest temptations luring us, as if by magic, to the little room on the roof. This was the Period of Austerity when foodstuffs were rationed. Coffee was expensive then and rare, but Binyamin would get it, I suppose, from some mysterious relative, and, anyway, no questions were asked. Coffee aside, Binyamin's contribution to the shaping of the Likrat group, both socially and artistically, was extremely important.

Natan Zach was a student of Dr. Baruch Kurzweill, then a teacher of literature at the well-known Reali High School in Haifa. Kurzweill later became a professor of literature at the newly established orthodox Bar Ilan University, but, even while teaching at Haifa, he was one of Israel's most important literary critics. Although they shared the same cultural Germanic background, something went sour between Zach and Kurzweill, for Zach would speak of his former teacher with pent-up hatred, notwithstanding some negative views they shared concerning the Palmach Generation writers.[4] That mystery aside, Zach had an indefinable charm that helped him become a leader. His charisma mixed authoritativeness with mystery, a life wisdom far beyond his years

---

[4]Writers who started publishing in the years immediately preceding the founding of the State of Israel.

with sharp intuition, and a cunning with a will that made it easy for him to exploit his adversaries' weak spots. Zach once brought to our meetings a sheaf of poems that, ironically enough, were stamped with the influence of Natan Alterman,[5] the very Alterman who would serve as the target of Zach's "War of Annihilation" of the late 1950s and 1960s. But who among us, with the possible exception of Binyamin, could boast of bearing no trace of Alterman's or Shlonsky's[6] influence? None.

The writers of the "Generation of the State" are presented as fiercely rebelling against Shlonsky's and Alterman's poetics, but their work did not emerge from a void—no literature does. Our clash with the preceding generation, the Palmach Generation, did not develop because of different sources of influence. Both they and we carried in our cultural knapsacks Alterman's *Stars on the Outside* and *Beggars' Joy* and Shlonsky's *Poems of Collapse and Conciliation*. It is true that a few of us rediscovered the early Uri Zvi Greenberg, Avraham Ben-Yitzhak, David Vogel, Yonatan Ratosh, and Avot Yeshurun—but the most powerful influence on our immediate predecessors as well as on ourselves was derived from an historic anthology titled *Russia's Poetry*. The volume, published in 1942, was edited by the poets Avraham Shlonsky and Leah Goldberg.[7] It was not reprinted for many years because Shlonsky's own Soviet orientation cast doubts on the selection of works and the editors' purpose. We revolted first against the orientation and its implications and later assailed the technical, formal expressions that characterized the approach.

One must point out that at the time the Likrat group evolved, most of the younger writers of the 1950s either belonged or were close to the greater Mapam (United Workers Party), which included two main wings—Hashomer Hatza'ir on the left and Achdut Ha'avoda on

---

[5]Natan Alterman (1910-1970), a brilliant craftsman, was the most influential Israeli Hebrew poet of the 1940s and 1950s.

[6]Avraham Shlonsky (1900-1973) led the modernist movement in Hebrew *belles lettres* in the 1920s, 1930s, and early 1940s.

[7]Avraham Ben-Yitzhak (1883-1950); David Vogel (1891-1944); Yonatan Ratosh (1908-1981); Avot Yeshurun (1904-1992); Leah Goldberg (1914-1970).

the right. Mapam, to the left of the ruling Israel Labor Party and mainly based on kibbutz movements, believed the Soviet Union to be the brightest beacon for the international proletariat. But Mapam tenaciously refused to accept the Soviet Union's brutal negation of Zionism. Culturally speaking, the literary and artistic mentors of Mapam worshipped Stalinist socialist realism. The critic Azriel Ukhmani was an archpriest of socialist realism, and the prominent novelists of the Palmach Generation, Moshe Shamir and Aharon Megged, lauded the style of life and the cultural characteristics of the Soviet bloc.

In addition to the literary supplement of *Al Hamishmar* [On guard], the party's daily newspaper, Mapam had a magazine for its young guard called *Bashaar* [At the gate]. Later, its younger writers founded a biweekly called *Massa*.[8]

The majority party in Israel's labor movement, Mapai (the Israel Labor Party), led by the state's founder, David Ben-Gurion, was anxious about Mapam's growing influence on young people and intellectuals. But the functionaries of both parties had the same mentality. To attract young writers to Mapai, the party funded a young guard's magazine, *Ashmoret* [Vigil] and a literary magazine, *Ayin* [Eye], edited by Nissim Aloni and Uri Sella. Formally, *Ayin* was published under the auspices of the Histadrut (the General Federation of Labor), but everyone knew where the money came from.

I published in both the Mapam and Mapai publications. But my opposition to the spiritual and artistic concepts of Mapam was absolute. Stalin's Soviet Union disgusted me, and I and my future colleagues on *Likrat* vehemently opposed socialist realism and the edict that made art subservient to ideology. We were, on the other hand, as passionately opposed to the Israel Labor Party's exaggerated pragmatism, its disrespect for intellectuals, and its identification with the bureaucratic and depersonalizing apparatus of the state.

The Likrat Group, as a whole, leaned left, but to an independent left, both anti-Soviet and anti-bureaucratic. I hedge by saying "as a whole" because this stance was not embraced by all. For example, Yehuda Amichai was well acquainted with Natan Zach. I didn't know him during the founding phase of Likrat, but my feeling is that the bridge between the two was built by cultural affinity—both were born in Germany and both admired Rilke and Lasker-Schiller. In any case,

---

[8]*Massa* can translate into English as either "burden" or "message."

when Stalin died, Amichai published in *Al Hamishmar* a poetic lament on the dictator's passing. No one else in our group would have dreamed of doing such a thing.[9]

Two tendencies, both carrying emotional and ideological weight, were paramount in the Likrat group. The "European" tendency, under the leadership of Harshav and Zach, strove to open windows to Western literature, then a sealed book to most of the younger writers. Aryeh Sivan and I chose the other tendency, which became known by the epithet "Native" (which I was only too happy to press into coin for our endeavor). At the time, Sivan was writing poetry with a distinct Canaanite flavor[10] as well as stories that were richly erotic. What I felt sharply were the psychological and emotional crises of the crumbling, intimate landscapes of the Motherland as it was swamped by waves of mass immigration. Neither Sivan nor I ever belonged to the Young Hebrew movement of Ratosh and Aharon Amir, and we didn't agree with them and their negation of Jewish history. At the same time, we were moved by an emotional Canaanism which was reflected in our writing. I also found a common ground with Nissim Aloni, a fine short story writer who later became one of Israel's most important playwrights, and I had taken to heart the collapse of *Ayin*, which had to fold because its two editors had gradually moved too far to the left.

Sivan and I would meet either at my parent's house, one of those that crowded the workers' quarters of what was then northern Tel Aviv,[11] at his widowed mother's apartment on old Dizengoff Street, or at various cafés. Those meetings, devoted as they were to intense liter-

---

[9]Amichai, born in 1924, served in the British army before joining the Palmach when the War of Liberation broke out. Defining writers by biographical criteria can be risky, but Amichai belongs both to the Palmach Generation and to the "Generation of the State" on the strength of this scant biography alone.

[10]Canaanite, in this instance, refers to a group of writers formally known as Young Hebrews and inspired and led by Yonatan Ratosh, who claimed that the natives of Israel, its indigenous people, comprised an entity separate from the Jewish people.

[11]Some people claim that there was a Tel Aviv Likrat group separate from the one based in Jerusalem. But this was not so: no literary clique rose from the shaded sand beneath the thick-leaved sycamores behind my parent's house.

ary debate, were filled with the enthusiasm of people who are beginning something, and they prepared us for the open and far more visionary nights in Jerusalem.

The trails leading to Likrat merged in Jerusalem.

We were constantly wandering between Jerusalem and Tel Aviv in search of work. Scholarship, and scholarships, were not enough. To feed myself, I took what jobs I could—from cleaner, janitor, and porter to editor and freelance journalist. Natan Zach took up night editing for the easy Hebrew daily, *Omer*, that was published for newcomers by the Federation of Labor. Harshav traded on his considerable talents by working as a private tutor. Pessach Meilin, later the copy editor (such titles did not exist then) of *Likrat* and related publications, was a proofreader at a printing press. Yehuda Amichai was, to the best of my knowledge, already a teacher. I cannot recall what sustained the young poet Gershon Shaked, now a professor at Jerusalem University; or Yigal Ephrati, who in time gave up poetry and joined the Department for the Support of Israeli Movies at the Ministry of Industry and Commerce; or Shaul Shaked, then a prolific essayist and now a well-known expert on Middle Eastern affairs. Yossef Bar-Yossef (who signed his stories "Yossef Bar"), a playwright and then the author of realistic stories about the lives of fishermen and seamen, found work as a sailor between semesters.

As hungry as we were, we mercilessly burned the days and nights and every free hour debating merely . . . everything. We were young, overflowing with hope, magnificently intoxicated by the biting, bright champagne that was youth.

Here are some lines I published 25 years ago:

In the days of our ebullient group, when we directly challenged the incumbent literary establishment—with all the credulity and faith of our youth—and strove to utterly demolish it, the relativity of time didn't exist—we would not have accepted it. Because at the very moment we acknowledged it, our youth would have been diminished. The worm of time would begin to gnaw at it—and we would be aware of that gnawing. Our offensive, so vibrant with youth, would lose its élan, enthusiasm, and sweep of vision. As a matter of fact, young poets defend their weak flank, that which is opposed by time, by demonstrations of fatigue, old age, and resignation which at times amaze the reader, who is unable to understand how such a feeling arises in young writers. But this is the dual view which is so human: while the young artist challenges his older colleagues in order to seize the plot of land vital for his development, he silences the voice of his own inner critic by psychologically identifying with failure and exhaustion, which are typical of the life experience and trials of people tottering under a burden of years much heavier than that of their challengers. These are two separate domains. While the bugles sound the attack, a sound lovely in its own insolence as the harbinger of change, the attacker laments the unmitigable sentence, the scythe of grandfather Chronus whose swish he catches with his sharp *inner* ear. And probably this may serve as an explanation for the intensity with which the artist takes possession of the experiences inspiring and advancing his creativity: he has no time. He senses the distant steps, the silent gnawing inside the walls. Therefore, the tired, anguished, and failing aspect of the writings of young people is not fake. Its authenticity is no smaller than that of the demonstration of youth, which is at times so brutal and inconsiderate—it merely depends on the observation post occupied by those who stand at the other side of the fence.

There was nothing fake about us. We assaulted with confidence the barricades of socialist realism, and the stagnant conservatism of the Association of Writers and its "eternal" functionaries. We searched vigorously for new means of expression and new linguistics and were insistent on preserving an *openness* toward all points of the compass in our effort to discover untrodden paths. We did what we did without pretense. If we were decadent, as some older critics charged, not one among us understood the term. What such critics mislabeled as decadence was, in fact, generative, all of it an expression of a youthful *joie de vivre* rising and flooding over the banks.

Again, the Likrat group's evolution was inevitable.

Ketuvim, *Turim*, and *Yalkut Hare'im*[12] came into being because their existence was inherent in the aspirations of the writers. When the first generation of writers born or raised in Israel emerged, an ebullience born of novelty, patriotism, and pride enabled the group to bask in the warmth of an enthusiastic welcome. When the next generation appeared, despite the fact that most of its members' personal histories were similar to those of the first group, it was greeted by a chorus of hostility and resentment. Why? Because those who stand in the spotlight and those who are trained to admire whatever is in that spotlight miss its familiar glare and warmth when it disappears.

Events could not have unfolded otherwise. We were unrestrained in our youth and exuberant enough to overlook the inattention.

Who was the first to conceive of publishing a periodical called *Likrat*?

The names of four editors appeared on the Likrat publications: H. Binyamin, Natan Zach, Aryeh Sirvan, and myself. No single person could wear the initiator's laurels. Our adventure was cooperative. For example, the manifesto of Likrat, stating the absolute independence of literature and negating any subservience to ideologues and ideologies, attests to the thoughts and imaginations of several people. Zach was responsible for finally polishing the manifesto, and I supplied the slogan, "Search for a new way!"—borrowed from Constantine Fofanov's poem, translated by Shlonsky in the previously cited volume *Russia's Poetry*.

"Search for a new way!" was, in essence, what we tried to express in those nights flooded by alcohol, and our unripe fiction, poetry, and polemics already contained the seeds vital for growth.

I haven't kept copies of our periodical, *Likrat*. The first two, stenciled publications—one in 40 copies, the other in 100—were given away or sold. (I don't remember the price, but the value can't be measured in money—we paid the expenses from our meager individual resources and sent it out into the world. Our attitude did not change when we switched to printing.)

Our first readers were young people, university students, beginning writers, and a few book-loving kibbutzniks. A very narrow circle. But

---

[12]*Ketuvim* [Texts], *Turim* [Columns], and *Yalkut Hare'im* [The friends' knapsack] were literary magazines serving as outlets for groups of Hebrew writers at various periods in Israeli history.

the reaction went beyond what one would expect from stenciled pages. The news got around, and the kind, warm-hearted words of readers cheered us no less than the shivers we felt on holding the first copies in our hands and turning the pages over and over and over.

The attacks came later.

The first barbs were launched by the left—we had, with a few articles, poems, and stories shocked the socialist realist establishment. As ridiculous as our efforts were judging by the appearance and circulation of our publications, Jerusalem's and Tel Aviv's hide-bound Marxists sensed danger.

The socialist realist publications were unanimous in harshly condemning us. We were denounced as uprooted nihilists, who, deaf to the demands of the times, were shirking responsibility. And other absurdities. Of course, they took full aim at our honest enough immaturity, but then it was not in their interest to let us mature.

I have already said that, chronologically, we were the *second* generation of Hebrew-language writers native to the State of Israel. As noted above, the first generation was, with all due regard, embraced because it was first. This positioning, however, did not lend it substance. The new literature was devoid of ideological threat. For all the hoopla, the first visionaries of the new state had taken aim at what was innocuous.

We were not so easily embraced.

We were not congratulated for existing.

No one was amused when we threatened established truths.

And our most voracious critics only made us more tenacious. We fed on their efforts to bury us, and instead of lying down, we dug in.

The Zionist socialist realists certainly stormed our trenches, but not without allies. The representatives of accredited, kosher Stalinism, spokespersons for the communist slaughterhouse, banged their blackened pots and polished their dull knives. I would not mention this—we attached no particular importance to it—but certain people believe in harnessing time to their carriages and changing both the length of the road and the account of their journey. They would erase from memory their alliances, their uncompromising hostility toward the rising shoots of our "Generation of the State" writing, and shape for themselves new faces for all the mirrors in which they would later be seen.

But that's all rubbish.

It was natural to expect an attack from Gabriel Moked, then a rising star among the younger generation of orthodox Marxist critics. Indeed, he was not late in launching it in the pages of *Kol Ha'am* [The people's voice], the daily newspaper published by the Israeli Communist Party in the early 1950s. I'm not sure whether Moked had graduated from high school at the time (for the sake of description, he was a thin fellow, dark-haired and tense, a survivor of the Holocaust whose shadows never stopped quivering across his face), but he was an authority on Marxist terminology. When he took us to task, in accord with all appropriate ideological laws and regulations in force, it was to issue a predictably scathing verdict of "Guilty!" He adamantly condemned the vagaries of Likrat even as his best friend, the young poet David Avidan,[13] flirted with our group in the wake of a rift that occurred between him and Alexander Penn, the veteran poet and literary editor of *Kol Ha'am.*

There was a story, perhaps with some truth in it, that Avidan's route from the Communist paradise was tied up in a personal clash with Penn. Avidan, who wrote revolutionary poems using typical Alterman-Shlonsky techniques, challenged the literary editor's authority by claiming that he, Avidan, was poetically more important. It's said that Penn physically kicked Avidan out of the editorial office, and the young poet's allegiance to the "world of progress" came to an end.[14]

The two stenciled publications of *Likrat* cast our reputation across the campus and into the cafés. A larger audience, primarily women and

---

[13]Moked and Avidan, both members of the Young Communist Guard, were students at Gymnasium Shalva in Tel Aviv.

[14]Avidan, exempted from military service because of his asthma, graduated from high school to study at the Hebrew University in Jerusalem and soon drifted into Likrat circles. He wanted to publish his first collection, *Lipless Faucets*, under Likrat's imprint. I can't clearly remember why that idea failed, but it may have been because Avidan refused to let Natan Zach, the editor of the Likrat books, go through his manuscript.

In 1954, when the book came out, it bore another imprint: Arad. Hard-pressed for money, the author had originally planned to publish his poems without vowels and in *plene* spelling (Hebrew words with additional vowels); Avidan, displaying a staggering agility, invented a literary ideology to justify this procedure. Finally, he discovered the needed funds and the book was published according to the best poetical tradition—that is, with vowels.

The idea of using *plene* spelling in Hebrew poetry has since vanished.

not limited to actual or potential writers, attended the public discussions and readings we held at residences or libraries.

Sivan was particularly happy about the changing composition of our readership.

When the first publication in print (rather than stencil) was issued, with a cover done by a well-known painter—Marian, a lonely, strange, tormented genius and ultimately a suicide—the audience became even more diverse. Sivan saw our public events as a double-edged sword, he himself gripping the handle, as the events both enhanced the reputation of our young literature and broadened the range of his female acquaintances. Not a few times did he slip from the edge of a literary evening, steeped in the smoke of cheap cigarettes and intoxicated by some local beauty whose lithe hands clung to his elbows. Our more serious members reacted adversely to this, finding such cavorting contrary to literary pursuits, but perhaps they were just jealous . . .

Sivan's gracefulness in these small affairs led at least once to serious conflict when he and Gershon Shaked happened to prize the same young woman, a tall, robust girl who had traveled to Israel with a youth *aliya* from Czechoslovakia, and who was not terribly interested in Hebrew literature. Sivan triumphed, but Shaked, in mute protest, sat out the night at the entrance to the house where Sivan was closeted with his Czech girl. It was raining, and the unlucky suitor got thoroughly wet, but still he did not give up.

Zach lived in an upper floor of an apartment building not far from Bezalel. The rooms were built in an eastern style, and the windows had wide niches in which one could settle and look out on Jerusalem. Books on art, literature, and philosophy were scattered everywhere, and sometimes Zach would disappear from the room, as if by magic. Some people swore that they saw him talking one moment: the next, he was gone, swallowed perhaps by the fog brushing against his window. At dawn, the fog dispersed, but the elusive Zach could not be found.

Regrettably, these disappearances were sometimes aggravating because Zach was supposed to bring manuscripts or express his opinion in discussions that were important to us. There were meetings that didn't take place because he, without notification or apology, didn't show up. In time, we learned to accept him as he was. Despite his eccentricities—somebody ascribed them, with a wink, to the fact that Zach had served in the Intelligence Corps during the war and, later on, in the reserves—he was able to immerse himself in bursts of intensive work. If it were not for Zach's persistence and dedication, Yehuda Amichai's first book of poems, *Akhshav U'bayamim Ha'akherim* [Now and in the other days], would never have been published by Likrat.[15] Amichai had departed for the United States, leaving his "poetical estate" in Zach's hands, and Zach selected, edited, and proofed the poems. His belief in the validity of Amichai's poetic values, which suited the new concept of poetry he was preaching, withstood all pressures.

The Likrat imprint also appears in *Broshim Levanim* [White cypresses], my first book and the first of the Likrat books, published in 1954. Later that year we published *Migdal Shemesh* [Sun tower], Moshe Ben-Shaul's first collection. Zach too was scheduled to publish his book, but couldn't make up his mind which poems to include. *Shirim Rishonim* [First poems] appeared in 1956, when the Likrat group was already a thing of the past. We pleaded with Zach to issue the book under the Likrat imprint, but he hesitated for a long time and finally refused. The publisher's name, as it appears on the appropriate page, is a strange one, comprising the Hebrew initials of a verse from Ecclesiastes: "Beware of producing many books." Zach's self-irony found a witty expression even in the name he used for his imprint.

Who financed the books?

It seems to me that we contributed whatever we could. The primary burden lay, naturally, on the author, but friends did their best to help. The principle we adopted was, if you can afford, give.

The same rule applied to the magazine. The third issue, which was the first to be printed and which bore the number "1," dangerously emptied our coffers. I've already described how we earned our living. Most of us belonged to families who were far from affluent. When the first copies of the new issue came out, we hawked them in the bohemian cafés of Jerusalem and Tel Aviv. When my book was published, we knocked on doors, offering copies to strangers, some of whom, perhaps shocked by our insolence, pulled out their wallets and paid up.

We also threw parties for our publications. The goods would be set on a side table and a fetching co-ed put in charge—and, wonder of wonders, our clientele yielded to either feminine or literary charms.

At such parties, we read our work and invited the audience to

---

[15]Amichai's book was published in 1955, nearly the last year of Likrat's existence.

express their views. There were many tough critics who tore our work
to pieces; but there was a respectable number of supporters as well.

The second printed issue of *Likrat*, bearing the number "2," was
nothing more than a booklet titled *Bishlosha* [In three]. It contained
poems by Natan Zach, Aryeh Sivan, and myself. On the cover appeared
a doe, drawn by the painter Menachem Geffen, who was very involved
in our affairs. His rented house in the Abu-Tur district served many
times as a venue for our meetings and celebrations. It was Menachem
who one day told us the good news about the publication of a selection
of Walt Whitman's poems in a Hebrew translation by Shim'on Halkin,
a poet who had come from America to teach literature at the Hebrew
University of Jerusalem. Menachem was very happy about the transla-
tion. He loved and admired Whitman immensely and demanded to
celebrate the event according to the best traditions of Likrat. We who
shared his love and admiration hurried to oblige him.

All night the party went on in an evacuated Arab stonehouse.
Even today, I remember Menachem's clear-voiced rhapsody as he read
from the translation:

> Poets to come! orators, singers, musicians to come!
> Not to-day is to justify me and answer what I am for,
> But you, a new brood, native, athletic, continental, greater
>   than before known,
> Arouse! for you must justify me.
>
> I myself but write one or two indicative words for the future,
> I but advance a moment openly to wheel and hurry back in
>   the darkness.
>
> I am a man who, sauntering along with fully stopping,
>   turns a casual look upon you and then averts his face,
> Leaving it to you to prove and define it,
> Expecting the main things from you.[16]

We all felt that the words of the poem were addressed to us, to all
of us.

---

[16]"Poets to Come." In *Walt Whitman: The Complete Poetry and Prose*.
New York: The Library of America, 1982, p. 175.

We financed *Bishlosha* as we had financed other publications—by scraping the bottom of the barrel, exerting ourselves to the maximum, and taking loans that we would repay from our meager earnings.

But, finally, we couldn't go on. We had entered a blind alley and we knew it.

Salvation arrived from the least expected direction.

In 1952, two Knesset members, David Livschitz and Channa Lamdan, had seceded from Mapam. They had belonged to the Achdut Ha'avoda faction of Mapam, representing the right wing of a leftist party. After seceding, they formed an independent faction in the Israeli parliament and launched a weekly publication entitled *Ma'avak* [Struggle]. They were joined by a group of intellectuals who had grown tired of Mapam's pro-Soviet orientation and disgusted with the frogs the party had to swallow because of that orientation: people like Dan Horowitz and Moshe Lissak, both of whom became professors at the Hebrew University in Jerusalem; the poet Ben-Zion Tommer; the essayist Mordechai Nissayahu; and others. Some time later, that group fell out with Livschitz, a brilliant intellectual and first-rate authority on the history of the international labor movement, but a difficult, morose, and foreboding man. The younger people moved away and the two ex-Mapamniks were left with their weekly.

The weekly was to be fed with appropriate material, from literature to politics. New, young people were desperately needed.

David Livschitz and Channa Lamdan, a pleasant woman and a true trade union organizer, had a young sympathizer, a genuine proletarian youth by the name of Yehuda La'yish. La'yish, destined to become the spokesman of the Ministry of Housing, was a theater enthusiast and in charge of theater criticism in *Ma'avak*. He also had a bosom friend, Yitzhak Livni, just recently graduated from high school and with literary aspirations; Livni would later stand at the helm of the Israel Broadcasting Authority for several crucial years. Livni wrote short stories and moved in Likrat circles. It was no wonder he introduced us, in Tel Aviv, to Yehuda La'yish. That gentleman approached us with a tempting proposition: *Ma'avak* would open its pages to us, granting us complete freedom of expression, and we would manage the literary supplement with full pay.

We convened among ourselves and held lengthy, soul-searching discussions. It was clear to us that financially we had reached the end of our tether: no longer could we secure the Likrat publications. We also needed a stage for our literary warfare.

We reached an agreement.

Zach became the literary editor of *Ma'avak* while I was appointed the managing editor of the weekly. Our salaries were ludicrous, but enabled us continue our literary activities for close to a year. And that was not all. The Livschitz-Lamdan faction financed another issue of *Likrat*, and we thanked our benefactors formally on the front page of the publication. I can testify that the faction did not interfere in either *Likrat* or in *Ma'avak*, and we were freely able to wage glorious battles against our enemies on the right and on the left, and on behalf of every literary phenomenon that merited our sympathy. We defended, for example, the outstanding poetry of Amir Gilboa, who had been attacked by conservative critics and by socialist realist pedants who intensely disliked his style.

The cover of our third printed issue of *Likrat* showed a drawing of a fisherman by the painter Yossi Stern. Like Menachem Geffen and Marian, Stern contributed the cover *gratis* "for the sake of our young literature."

Likrat's activities moved to a large extent, then, to Tel Aviv. I myself had left Jerusalem in the summer of 1952. Zach and Sivan stayed on in Jerusalem, to the best of my recollection, for another year. Herushovsky-Harshav and Shaked settled in Jerusalem.

But surprises, out of all proportion to the limited circulation of our magazines and books, never stopped.

Thus it happened on one of those evenings at the Alexander Moses printing press (near the Tel Aviv Central Bus Station) where *Ma'avak* was printed, that a young man, muscular and tanned, wearing sandals and shorts, showed up brimming with ideas. This was Anadad Eldan, who had begun publishing his first poems that year, 1953. A former Palmachnik and a product of Kibbutz Hepzibba near the historic Mount Gilboa, he had found his way to us. Along some mysterious route, a copy of *Likrat* had arrived at his doorstep at the kibbutz, and he got it into his head to meet us, with the affinity of spirit that drives writers to certain literary families that are their natural homes.

Eldan opened his mouth the moment he entered the press, and after a hasty "Shalom," erupted into topics that were of great importance to him, all above the roar of the printing machinery. Zach and I felt the same—this man from the kibbutz was boiling over with words that had been heating up for years.

The feeling was precisely the same when the three of us—Zach, Sivan, and I—arrived at Café Stern on Dizengoff Street in Tel Aviv to introduce ourselves to the poet Avot Yeshurun, formerly Yehiel Perlmutter, one of the most original shapers of modern Hebrew verse. With his mane of hair cascading above his thin body, he seemed completely isolated from the café's other customers. His eternal cup of tea was growing cold on the table. We approached, excused ourselves (he raised his dark, introspective eyes, as if drawn back from an immense distance), and let flow the many thoughts that had been pressing in us for release. We had read his book (at that time his only book), *Al Khakhmot Drachim* [On the wisdom of roads], already published in 1942, and loved it. We also liked his new poems that were so viciously attacked in the press. Why did we go to him? Because of the same affinity of spirit that had driven Anadad to us. Yeshurun was a unique poet, endowed with a singular, original voice. The offensive waged against him in those days centered on the ideological content of his poetry as interpreted by establishment critics, who were inevitably short-sighted in their cogitations, and it drove us to span the age gap.

I don't remember whether Avot Yeshurun or Anadad Eldan attended the party held on the occasion of the publication of my book, *Broshim Levanim*, the first of the Likrat books. We gathered on the bank of the Yarkon River to celebrate the event. The poet Abraham Huss, later a professor of meteorology at the Hebrew University in Jerusalem, published a sympathetic full-page critique in *Massa*.

Life then was full of surprises.

We drank a lot, talked a lot, sang a lot. Our sweet-hearts were beautiful, so beautiful we became mute looking at them. The breeze, swaying the tops of the eucalyptus trees on that clear night, brought tidings which could not be defined but were overflowing with promises.[17]

Translated by James Oppenheim

---

[17]In this memoir, I have only briefly touched on what might be called "the poetics of Likrat." I'm not sure we Likrat people had a clear-cut, definitive poetic theory at that time. Perhaps it's more correct to say that we were driven by an uneasy feeling about the existing literary situation and the growing consciousness of "having to do something different." This, of course, contradicts the manifesto put forth in our first publication. Well, life is always stronger than manifestoes. But that's another story.

The Alley

Honestly, it was an escape. I'd be the last to deny it. Still, when I feel low, I close my eyes, and sometimes I find myself back in that little Parisian street whose name I don't remember. I float and glide in a dreamy silence between two walls of trees that cast a greenish, dense shade on old cobblestones. And now I feel a sudden dread that it's all a dream inspired by excessive yearning. But no, that cannot be, because I really was there, though not by design. The fact is, I don't remember the name of that alley, defended by two hedges of heavy-topped trees, an alley that seemingly sailed on water. And the trees—very old trees indeed—were they box, elm, linden? Curiously enough, I'm sure they weren't chestnut trees, although chestnuts are so typical of Paris. I don't have any proof, only a feeling of quiet assurance. That feeling gripped me immediately on entering that alley, where I arrived under vague circumstances.

Yes, I'm sure it wasn't planned at all. It happened. Just like that. I was wandering about and suddenly found myself there, at that very alley, on a summer or maybe an autumn morning, the green shade filling the air like a wave, and silence embracing it, inseparable.

If you ask me when all this happened, I don't know. Maybe 30 years ago, maybe not so long. At that time, I seldom traveled abroad. Those who don't travel often are more likely to retain details of their journeys. Those who travel often among foreign landscapes can find it difficult to distinguish the numerous images mingling in memory. It's easy to contradict what I write: if I didn't travel much, you'd think I'd remember the name of the street, its beginning and end, the quarter where it was located, the streets leading into it. But I don't. I do remember the good, peaceful solitude of protective trees, the green shade, the silence.

I'm certain I arrived there in the morning. On that visit to Paris I stayed at a small hotel in the Latin Quarter. I would rise early to wander about the city on my own, either by *métro* or on foot. Because writing is both my trade and passion, I naturally hunt for places that are somehow related to literature. It was the same in Paris. Thus, from time to time I came upon a house or street or café connected to a certain writer or book. I'd be seized with joy and want to cry aloud, "Land Ahoy!" like a sailor in his crow's nest who spies the thin line of solid earth after many days and nights perched between water and sky.

But that street or alley had nothing to do with literature. It was uncontaminated by language, existing in its own green, lush silence. A morning hour, either summer or autumn; a clear sky spread over the abundant shade, over the foliage, the pale azure light shimmering like a pearl. And yet the street was saturated with the kind of silence that floods the ears after, not before, the storm. A peaceful and confident sea, yet moved by some current more powerful than its own. An intimacy born of mutual respect, not fear. Intimacy without insistence. And more—a deep, omnipresent, and forgiving love. A sea at dusk, at the close of a day's bustle. That very sea flowed there in the alley, in the morning, amazing and wondrous.

The whole time I spent in that alley, I was free of allusions. This I remember well—the absence of mental exertion. A writer is not only haunted by literary associations, but exists in a dimension of incessant spiritual tension, always searching for subject matter, possibilities, solutions. This tension is not bound to immediate expression, but it's always there, unrelenting, that desperate search for sounds, colors, smells. Which will later be cast in words. On that street, I found myself shedding the neurosis of creativity. The builder in me dropped his tools and thirstily drank the silence, the fullness, the marvelous unity of something beyond explanation, interpretation, beyond form and shape—a supreme green.

Later, back in my own country, I read a poem by Y. Z. Rimmon, "An Evening Slumbering Over the Sea." I was struck by its strange affinity to what I had experienced in that Parisian alley. That's probably why I like the poem so much:

> An evening slumbering over the sea. Following
>   a sky pale as an adolescent dream,
> A miraculous red, like the fire of youth, dawn,
>   and then silence.

A lonely star, which peeped at me like a star
        of boyhood, I missed it.
Now I listen to the noise of the sea, and it
        listens to the silence of my heart,
        like my friend.
God is over me like the walls of garden trees
        washed in night's light,
And my heart ponders over far expanses of sea
        and its distant paths . . .
I think: A seer's youth is like a sea and the
        length of all his days is like a sea—
and what is it between sea and sea, when God is
        unfathomable yet makes Himself visible?

Much later, I found myself once again driven by the inevitable
need to trace the artistic-verbal parallel to what is beyond expression,
that malediction that is sometimes too heavy to bear (and this truth
each artist discovers with ripening time, not in the morning of youth)
. . . but how beautiful then the sense of liberation, of absolute ease, of
removing the familiar burden off aching shoulders!

Green, green—nothing to do with Lorca's somnambulists—and si-
lence, silence. Where are those trees? Where is that peace floating over
worn cobblestones? Where is the silence, the rest, the place where one
can keep one's eyes open with no fear of confrontation?

Where is that street?

Where is that city?

Was it a figment of my imagination?

No, it was real. It happened. It must have happened. I must have
sailed over a serene sea with my legs planted firmly on the pavement,
sailing and soaring, at ease and believing, free and victorious, confident
and loving.

What else does a writer need?

What else does a man need?

And that's why there is such a retreat, with its extravagant trees,
their splendid foliage. I'm both witness and judge. My verdict cannot
be appealed. Listen: my ears are overflowing with a green silence. All
maps are redundant. All alleys are open. That alley was never blind.

Translated by Barbara Goldberg

65

My Father

The year before my father died, he was seized by memories of his childhood and youth. If the events of recent years blurred in detail, the stories of his growing up in the town of his birth, Mogilev on the Dnieper River, would grip him in a luminous hold.

My father was part of the third *aliya*,[1] but it was not these years that would call to him or that seemed to hold him in thrall; rather, he returned to the earlier days, such as the years before the revolution when he studied at a Russian high school. He vividly remembered the uniform he used to wear, the snug fit, the brass buttons, the peaked cap that he drew down over his forehead. On one occasion, when he was at the theater (he may have been fifteen years old), Czar Nicholas entered with his entourage—the audience stood up in unison, as though they had been rehearsed for this possibility for years—and turned as if on cue in the direction of his Imperial Majesty. Did they sing the national anthem, "God Save the Czar"? He didn't say, and I did not think to ask.

He spoke of how during the First World War, Czar Nicholas moved the General Staff to his home town. One day during winter the royal family passed in the streets. On sleds or in car, I may have asked? Though my father answered excitedly, as if taken by my interest, it is my memory that fails. I can no longer say. He stood on the sidewalk, his head bare because he had taken off his cap despite the bitter cold, and stared at the autocrat, the autocrat's wife, the daughters, and the

---

[1]The wave of Jewish immigration, or *aliya*, to Palestine between 1919 and 1924 was composed mainly of young pioneers from communist Russia and other territories comprising the new Soviet Union, which had declared an ideological war against Zionism and the Hebrew language.

heir, a sickly boy of ten or eleven. How many imagined that in a few years three centuries of Romanov despotism would evaporate as though they had never occurred, and that royal blood would run in the streets, no different from common blood?

My father was a member of a Zionist-socialist movement and never, as a young man, felt even a shade of affection for the autocrat. Still, his eyes clouded as he spoke of Nicholas, or of the trappings of czarist rule. Why did this period of life so compel him? And why in such a way? I cannot say. I would try to listen attentively, but I was unable to ask him deeply personal questions. He would intimately discuss Grand Duke Nicholas Nikolayevitch, the Czar's uncle, a rabid Jew-hater and commander-in-chief of the Russian army until deposed by order of his nephew, who seemingly took the rein of state into his own hands. My father spoke of the affair as if he were personally involved, weighing the pros and cons and passing judgment, which differed from time to time when he retold the story.

Despite this extraordinary return to the past, my father still remained a mystery. I have facts, of course. I knew where he was born and how he stealthily crossed the White Russian-Polish frontier, with a band of pioneers, to travel to the Land of Israel. I also knew about the beginning of his experiences there, and even something about the later days. Beyond that, I knew almost nothing. Certainly not about intimate episodes in his life and less so of the intimacies of his struggling. In truth, he was a sealed book, and still is. We never had extensive conversations and certainly never a soul-to-soul talk. Our whole lives, we traveled separate roads. Neither he nor I broke through the other's ego. We lacked the strength. Even what one of our writers calls "the thorny existence" remained out of bounds, though ordinarily human beings are more than grateful for a sympathetic ear in times of trouble. Even while suffering, we kept our doors locked. Those cords of darkness, twisting between father and son, ties that go beyond logic and reason, feeding on the crumbling cells of the body—these bonds probably were the only ones that existed, that still exist, but what do I know of my father in the light?

> And what of your alien son yearning
> to mine deepest space, to chart galaxies
> more distant than lunacy, than love?

And why do I write these verses (from the poem "Father") when I am able to say so little about the man? In one sense, it is quite simple. Recently, I read *Minsk: The Mother City*, two volumes about a Jewish community in White Russia which for hundreds of years had a rich, busy life, producing many renowned scholars, though few today would recognize their names. All of this—the Jews of renown and the ordinary Jews—came to an end with the Holocaust. And yet there are the two volumes, written with profound care. Some of those who lent a hand to this enormous undertaking are no longer among the living. The editor, a veteran member of Kibbutz Sadeh Hachum in the Beissan Valley, fortunately still is.

Well, *Minsk: The Mother City* is the reason for these words.

My father was neither born in Minsk nor raised there, though he lived nearby. Jews first settled in his home town, straddling both banks of the Dnieper, in the 16th century. While he had nothing to do with the compilation of the volumes, he nevertheless has a small foothold in Volume Two: it is a brief memoir, published under his name and the title "Minsk as a Station on the Way to the Land of Israel." In that memoir, my father writes how he and his pioneer friends arrived in Minsk and remained until they were able to steal across the border into Poland, which was not far. Acting on the recommendation of Peretz Markish, the great Yiddish poet, they had gone to Minsk to study at the Yiddish Institute, which had been founded there.

Avraham Shlonsky, a member of their group who later sparked the modernist school of Hebrew poetry in Israel, asked Markish to help them. For them, though, the studies were a charade: I hardly remember my father writing or uttering even one word in Yiddish. He had been educated in Russian and Hebrew. Still, they needed a permit to remain in Minsk, and it was granted because of their enrollment at the Institute. My father had never spoken of this adventure or of this period of his life. I didn't know, for example, that he and Shlonsky's brother-in-law had been appointed as foremen in a group of turf diggers. This was their livelihood until they succeeded in smuggling themselves across the border. "We had to supply 1000 cubic meters of turf to the power station in Minsk," my father writes. "We would dig the turf out with shovels, extricate blocks of turf 20 centimeters thick, put the blocks out to dry like bricks, and when dry we would carry the turf in a wagon to town. We had a wagon with two horses."

I have imagined how my father struggled with his job. My mother once told me, after his death, and as if against her will, of the time my father spent in the building industry, after they had arrived in Palestine. How he used to return home when night had already fallen, the palms of his hands wounded and swollen. How he would drop down totally exhausted. Naturally, he never spoke of it. In the *Minsk* memoir, he writes of his turf digging: "How was I given such a job? I studied at the Faculty of Mining at the university. When I applied for work at the proper White Russian department, the director was happy to have me. He thought I was an accomplished mine engineer. Actually, I didn't know anything about turf digging, but a Jewish expert worked at that office . . ." In short, the expert had a sensitive ear, was secretly a Zionist, and my father confided in him. He told him about their group in Minsk and of their intentions to get to Palestine. The expert helped them to carry off their pretense and instructed my father on what he had to do as a turf digger.

I knew my father had been a university student before he made *aliya*, but I knew nothing about his mining career. He did not tell me anything about that. After his death, my mother spoke of how she had pleaded with him to continue his studies at the Technion, the technical college in Haifa. He adamantly refused. In the biographical note in *Minsk*, my father is characterized as a "pioneer worker." He himself wrote there a fabulous tale about a young Jew, formerly a schoolmate of Shlonsky's, who served in the communist political police and almost turned my father's group in. But the young Jew thought the better of it. He made *aliya* at the same time as my father, stealthily crossing the Soviet-Polish border and going on to Palestine. There he became a pioneer worker, joining the Labor Brigade,[2] and drifted to the left. Finally, he left for the Soviet Union, but the Soviet authorities refused him reentry. Ignoring his passionate pleas, they ordered him to stay in Italy, where he became active in the Italian Communist Party. Later he studied chemistry in Paris and became a noted scientist, even participating in a scientific conference at the Weizmann Institute in Rehoboth and lecturing at the Hebrew University in Jerusalem.

I heard that story from my father but only by chance, after he read an interview I did with Shlonsky, in which there were, according to my father, a few inaccuracies. Why did he choose to tell me about the

---

[2] A pioneering organization of idealistic Zionist socialists in the days of the third *aliya*, paving roads, draining swamps, and building kibbutzim in Palestine.

mysterious scientist and not about himself, about his wanting to become a mining engineer, about his digging turf and getting his palms bloodied, about my mother pleading with him to enroll at the Technion, and about his stubborn refusal?

I don't know, of course. And I did not ask. What remains are only "bonds of rage and blind, hot weeping / woven not here and terminated not at this place" (Natan Alterman). And the borders that I still cross secretly in a hard, mad country, borders without a beginning or end . . .

My father's memoir in the *Minsk* volume has a photograph of him and his friends. It was taken at the final stop before crossing the Soviet border. The people in it are marked by numbers—in vain have I tried to identify my father's face by his number. It is too blurry. All my attempts have ended in failure.

Translated by Merrill Leffler

In Kaestner's Footsteps

In one of his famous "Emil" stories for children, the German author Erich Kaestner tells how he would ride the train to neighborhoods far from the one where he lived. There, in those strange, unfamiliar quarters, an intense feeling of loneliness would well up in him. Close on the heels of loneliness came a longing to return to his home turf. Thus washed in yearning, he would trace his way back to his "origins." Reading between the lines, we sense that this tension between womb and wanderlust helped fuel Kaestner's creativity.

I would often think of Kaestner and his questing train trips when traveling from Tel Aviv to Jerusalem to write poetry. Finding my pressure-cooker existence in the town of my birth to be bad for writing, I would "go up," as we say, to Jerusalem. We mean that phrase both figuratively and literally, for one must indeed embark on a steep ascent from Sha'ar Ha'gai (the Gate of the Valley) through a spiral of wooded hills in order to reach that most profound and sacred of cities.

Sha'ar Ha'gai served as a gate through which I passed from one time to another, from one existence to another. Through the window I would note the change in the landscape, a kind of transmutation: trees would change into other trees, plants to other plants, stones and soil into other stones and soil. The quality of the air, too, would noticeably change, from damp and dense to cool and light.

Upon reaching Jerusalem, I would find that the people had changed as well. Their faces, clothing, manners, figures of speech, even their ways of thinking were all different here on the mountaintop than in that gritty city along the coast.

And after setting foot upon Jerusalem soil, I would, like Kaestner, wander away from the neighborhoods I habitually frequented, finding myself in places like Beit Hakerem or the German Quarter, places which would pour into me a sweet, intoxicating strangeness. The shock of that strangeness, and the yearning it provoked, choked me. Thus alienated, I would begin writing poetry.

A similar but more powerful feeling of alienation would overtake me in foreign lands. The Land of Israel, that marvelously lively essence of tastes and scents, colors and vistas, would beckon to me from far away. My poems were bridges, stretched to the shape of my native landscape.

Why do I elaborate on that point? Because it has become evident to me that, as I grow older, the scope of my horizons does not expand but retracts. The reality of my motherland gradually becomes more tangible, less abstract. Distant lands retreat before the Land of Israel. Jerusalem retreats before Tel Aviv. The city retreats before the small town. Under the tarmac the earth becomes more earthy. The grass becomes more grassy in its shrinking spot of soil. The water becomes more watery in its accumulating, introspective flow.

My circuit has come to its close. No longer must I travel even to the outskirts of a metropolis. It is enough to go from one street to another. From one neighbor's house, with its small plot of land, to the next.

Translated by Marilyn Millstone

Part Two

Poetry:

More Distant than Lunacy, than Love?

Father

My brown-eyed father studied
mine engineering before he came
to a good land and a large, a land
flowing with milk and honey, whose stones
are iron and out of whose hills
thou mayest dig brass.

What did he hope to find buried
in the belly of the earth, what
minerals, what precious ore hidden
from his brown eyes? He waded
bare-legged in bitter swampwater
rustling with bulrushes. Roadbuilders'
pickaxes shattered plain rock.

Out of pagan cardboard skies a fiery
star plummets: Icarus,
your alien son, sinks into the abyss
on molten wings of wax, shattering
the dream of redemption.

For years my father was confined
to a desk job, the echo of pickaxes,
of rustling water, growing faint
as though muffled by cottonwool.
His brown eyes stared dully
at walls where frustration flickered
in the lantern light, his inner ear
hearing the sweet sound of pickaxes
striking veins of coal. Returning home

late at night, my father felt pits gape
underfoot, like the emptiness
beneath a mountain's ribs.

And what of your alien son yearning
to mine deepest space, to chart galaxies
more distant than lunacy, than love?

My father digs, he digs, fails
to test the soil's layers for hot springs
about to gush forth, his eyes
brown agates, his knuckles, iron,
the geology of a fatherland crumbling
in the socket of his hip.

Father, manganic acid reddens the shales
of my brown eyes. How shall I ever
find peace in this sandstone?

Over the earth's corpse stretch roads
of latitude and roads of longitude,
bulrushes shrivel in the parched land,
the maps of stars are swallowed up
by the void and the dust which is
my father, dustfather, practices a new
kind of mine engineering, perhaps
in a chosen land. Or one that is not.

Translated by Barbara Goldberg

In the Absence of a Motherland

Without a spiritual motherland
it is the Israel of blood the soul loves:
on the roof the washing embraces the wind,
the message of snow is carried from the mountains,
in the yard oleanders sense the water
and the sun crowns the burning head with a tiara
     of thorns.

In the absence of a spiritual people
the beloved is Israel of flesh and blood:
a dark child rends the sea,
tamarisks turn to salt on the lips,
arak[1] pours over a Jerusalem of stone
and your thigh is sweet at a time neither day
     nor night.

Without a language of the spirit
Israel of blood is multiply loved:
the red breast of a watermelon ripped open,
the acacia hedge bathes in gold
and when noontide slumbers,
on the glass of the horizon, the bird
of your heart knocks softly to be admitted.

Translated by Myra Sklarew

---

[1]An alcoholic drink made from anise popular in the Middle East.

Deserters

Even those who desert, if Hebrew was their
first cry of life, carry in the secret of their inner flesh
a little Yarkon,[1] two or three Jerusalem stones or
a hoeful of heavy, crumbling
clods of Emek[2] earth.

Here, in this house of light, among success
stories in a strange tongue whose accent betrays
different water and mountains, suddenly their heart
stops beating in this time dimension. Indeed,
if somebody, following a belief of earlier days, had
taken a photograph of the frozen pupils of their
eyes, the photo would have exposed
the murderer in the shape of a little Yarkon, two
or three Jerusalem stones or a hoeful of
heavy, crumbling clods of Emek earth.

Translated by Myra Sklarew

---

[1]A river crossing Tel Aviv.

[2]The Valley of Jezreel in the north of Israel.

Town

The town of my birth is the town where
I live, my guarantee against the anxieties
of immigrants, through whose fingers
time flows like sand in an ordinary wind.

Why, then, when the mulberries
unscroll their sticky bright sprouts
am I filled with nostalgia for towns
where I wasn't born, won't ever live?

Translated by Laura Fargas

Mulberry Leaves

Mulberry leaves can only protect us
so far. When the seams crack,
shelter is lost. And what of the sun bleeding
in the tendons, in the grain of the leaves?
It too will whiten like a stripe of white paint
on a new wall in the foremost Hebrew town, then
yellow, like that same stripe on an aging wall.
Mulberry leaves can only protect us
so far.

Translated by Jean Nordhaus

Camels

The sand sings with little hollow
mouths, its protest
on this ravished beach.

Who listens to it?
Yet it continues
its tiny song of protest
under the cement pillars
and fortifying iron girders.
The God of Sand takes it down
in his private notebook
somewhere in the Sahara, probably.
And like a secret agent, a faint
moon sneaks up and peeps
out from a high collar
of clouds. Sand climbs
invisible ladders of light,
drops of sound too pure
to be absorbed, nets of cruel
salt. Floating across
on broad soft hooves, caravans
of phantom camels traverse
pillars and molds. The sand
sings. The light drips. The salt
gnaws. Caravans pass. And I
listen.

Translated by Elaine Magarrell

Roots

God decreed that every man must live in the country
where his roots are. Like a growing tree
which dies when uprooted and transplanted
in another place, so a man's soul stops growing
when uprooted from the place of its roots.

Alexandr Solzhenitsyn, U.S.A., 1976

He who keeps track by pain doesn't need
divine guidance to know where the roots are.
Like a void left by an amputated arm,
what we miss hurts, not what we have.
In a green country rustling with plenty
of water, I count grains of lean sand
roasted by a demented sun, the same sun
which stood over Gibeon or Tel Aviv
in order to scorch maps of fire in tree-
tops, tree-trunks and even in roots.

Translated by Elaine Magarrell

Lot's Wife

Lot's wife looked back and turned
into a pillar of salt. Why did she look?
Was it an irresistible urge toward
suicide—a drunk husband and two
opinionated daughters—or her ties
to the motherland, going up in flames?
We'll never know. Even today, those arriving
at the Dead Sea's coast can, if they really try,
discern (or perhaps imagine) something
there, an eroded human face on that celebrated
pillar of salt. Anyway, the lesson has not
been learned: too many of us cannot control
the urge to look backward and so
our land is strewn with avenues of salty
pillars, white monuments, like Rodin's
sculptures whose faces froze in expressions
of longing, wrath, despair, hope, resignation—
but always nipping the tongue with saltiness.

Translated by Catherine Harnett Shaw

Tasmania

Press Item: The Australian government encourages emigration to Tasmania

Poets go into exile from interior exile. Tasmania
is an island separated from the southeastern horn
of Australia by 130 kilometers at the narrowest point
of the shallow Bass Straits. The original
population, curly-haired Negroes, flat-nosed and thick-
lipped, comprised an anthropologically distinct group
and were entirely decimated around the mid-19th century.
Whites came after them, originally criminals exiled
from their motherland. The distance between our continent
and Tasmania is much greater than 130 kilometers, but pressures
are mounting steadily and poets go from inner exile into
exile, though they are neither anthropologically distinct nor
criminals, and the land of exile is the motherland.
The original population of Tasmania, Negroes with curly hair,
flat noses, and thick lips, were decimated before
they had time to write poetry. Whites came after them,
while in our continent, poets go into exile from a deeper
exile by the shallow waters of the Yarkon River.
The Bass Straits, even at their narrowest, remain
beyond the concept of the poem.

Translated by Jean Nordhaus

Skinheads

Skinheads invade the small familiar
garden, light beaming
off their shaven scalps.

They shoot at the birds
with slings, kick the raked
leaves, their derisive laughter
destroying the sun's symmetrical palaces.

How old you've grown, Orpheus, on your bench
screened by the barren fruit trees, dreaming
of the eternal virgin, Eurydice, while
goldfinches light on your long, whitening hair.

When the skinheads rush past him, Orpheus
moans in his sleep. They don't even glance
in his direction: ancient history, music
nobody wants to listen to these days.

Translated by Elaine Magarrell

Even a Small Garden

Even a small garden, when darkness falls,
suddenly has a dimension of depth.
Listen how the sifting wind
carefully picks leaves of deceit, of fidelity.

Translated by Laura Fargas

Bamboe

The plaque in the nursery reads: *Bamboe*.
One word meaning bamboo.
Noontide, so non-Dutch
in its warmth and azure, on the bank of the traditional canal.
My eyes read: *Bomb* time and again.
What can one expect from such Mediterranean eyes?
They insist, though I repeatedly correct
the visual error, on deciphering the world in their own way.
Just as they see on the street of our fathers
a sudden explosion carve gaping mouths
into the dark brown stones, mouths
muttering Holy Holy even when the blood
is burning their voices.

Amsterdam, 1989

Translated by Myra Sklarew

Summer 1982[1]

Love's game is sweet in a burning noon
scented with pine. Smoke blossoms
drift over the city. You are still
a girl. I'm still a boy.

And a hoarse voice shouted that a city
was dying. A delicate column of smoke
swayed in the distance. You are still
a girl. I'm still a boy.

And somebody softly recited poetry.
A soft touch of lips, refusing to acknowledge anything
else, shut out the world. You are still
a girl. I'm still a boy.

Fresh coolness of art
in that burning noontide. Pine scent
blue as smoke. You are still
a girl. I'm still a boy.

Light quicker than thunder.
Maybe a big gun, maybe a lucky
image of a city stabbed to death by a poem.
You are still a girl. I'm still a boy.

Translated by Henry Taylor

---

[1]The Lebanese War broke out in June 1982.

Shelter

We cleaned out the bomb shelter,
a municipal edict too stringent
to ignore. We worked diligently:
an iron bedstead with protruding springs,
broken utensils, a scrap of mirror,
a plastic container whose contents
had evaporated long ago, the junk
of life, all collected and dumped.

Now that the shelter has been restored
to its original condition, we are filled
with a sense of our own virtue, cleansed
of sloth and regret. Now we can wait
for evil from any direction. Only
our image reflected in that sliver
of mirror is slightly blurred, perhaps
because we have let down our guard.
How quickly dust accumulates on the glass.

Translated by Barbara Goldberg

In the Time of Creative Barrenness

What is at fault is the time of creative barrenness.
If it were possible to imagine what would ripen, like
a terrible fetus, in love's womb, or how the city, that
executioner, would extend long arms of smoke; if it
were possible to build, in a lowly garden smeared
with babies' cries even more than with fallen leaves,
palaces of pale silver; if we had a myth
where roots suck rage from the earth's lean breast; then
perhaps things would have been different.
But in the time of creative barrenness what does the sea
mumble with senile lips of tar and algae,
what cataract darkens the moon's eye,
what craving fills the politician's soul
when he tosses in his bed on the coastal plain,
while fog climbs up his windows, and he is exposed
to all the season's influences, and beyond,
to the mountains that may possibly be there?

Translated by Henry Taylor

Balance of Power

Please don't misunderstand. Poetry cannot
topple regimes. In the squares,
on the barricades, the ardent young
recited lines, even verses, from their favorite
poems. But only before the tanks
rolled in. Later they fell silent.

Anyhow, when the Secretary General stepped
out of the limousine (his chauffeur
hurrying to open the door) he felt
dusk dripping on his lips
like drops of a thin, lilac rain.

For that moment, was there a balance
of power? Hard to say. It seemed
as though he paused briefly, and then
pulled down the brim of his hat
in order not to get wet.

Translated by Barbara Goldberg

Directions

When the Caliph Ummar ibn el-Khatab, a pure Bedouin, orders
the burning of the Great Library of Alexandria—"if the books parrot
the Koran they are redundant; and if they contradict,
it is virtuous to destroy them"—his thin lips tighten, almost
disappear, his swarthy skin as dry as Arabian dunes, his hawk-like
Semitic nose. The wideness of water makes him nervous. That is why
he turns his back on the Mediterranean, pinkened
by sunset, soon turning red as the flames
devour smooth papyrus. Only the poets see
letters, birds or souls take flight from the raging
fires consuming epics, discoveries. "There is no God
but Allah and Mohammed is the Prophet of God," he says kneeling
on the small, plain rug, no ornament to distract
the mind, seduce the sense, and he finds that in the dancing
light it is so easy to direct
the face toward Mecca.

Translated by Catherine Harnett Shaw

Jericho

Tonight Rahab's scarlet thread marks
her windowsill again like a trail
of congealed blood, while a Jericho
frozen in moonlight and ancestral
silence, awaits the trumpets' blast.

And in the poinciana, fireflies flare
like torches in the eyes of stupefied
ass and ox and sheep, whose slaughter,
swift and absolute, shall be exacted
by human hands, at God's decree.

Translated by Barbara Goldberg

Assimilation

An evening steamy as a Chassidic bathhouse.
Between your breasts, coastal plain, your sweat
drips like blood which cannot clot. Soon
the incoming breeze will offer a small
consolation. Under the asphalt, bones
of Canaanite, Philistine, Hebrew
and Arab assimilate, and possibilities
forbidden by Mosaic law shall secretly
fertilize the promised land.

Translated by Barbara Goldberg

Jonah II

No, not like Jonah trying to flee
God's embassy to an alien nation;
not in that ship, about to be broken up
in our Mediterranean, survivors and sleepers
roused—once the storm is past—
to join in our prayers. Not, it's only
a simple escape—maybe stupid,
surely absurd at an age when people
are ending, not beginning things—to simplicities:
warmth of a palm; eyes that darken and clear;
the echo of a moan; scent of shampooed hair; pleasure
and satiety so common, they won't even
be mentioned in a footnote for future scholars.
And what of the motherland? Now especially
when autumn bends so limpidly
to comfort her?

So we go back to the beginning:
Prophets aren't the only ones allowed
to pick the proper season for a getaway.
Ordinary mortals—even poets—
are sometimes smart enough to give the right answer
when waking to find themselves on the deck
of a historic ship or in a bedroom
lacking exceptional character.

Translated by Jean Nordhaus

Against Memory

Wrapped up in you I search
for peace. More precisely: escape.
Sniffing your armpit, I grow hard
like a wall against memory, invasive
dreams, a motherland crumbling
like stones, dripping like sand
in an hourglass from some old
curiosity shop. You don't understand
why I dip my fingers in your sweat, inhale
with desperate lust. When you draw them close
to your nose, you smell only a trace
of shaving cream, something
pleasant, ordinary, masculine,
of no political meaning, especially
under such a circumstance.

Translated by Catherine Harnett Shaw

If I Forget You

Man is only the reflection of his native landscape.

Shaul Tchernichovsky

I was asked how I could write native
poems in a foreign land. I answered
what I answered. I didn't say my right hand
never forgot how to cross the no-man's land
between your buttocks, that my left travels
free along the borderline, that gorge
between your breasts, and when digging—a stubborn,
weathered archeologist—in your tunnel, I was
bound to find that layer under which looms
the honeyed essence of my native land.

Translated by Catherine Harnett Shaw

In the Big Country

America is like a too-big hat on me,
sliding over my forehead, my eyes.
Even when I shake back

my head, yank the brim, it still
doesn't fit, like that
time in Kansas City,

my right foot in one state, my left
in another, and the heart,
that stupid puppy, strained and bounding

up that hill, wanting more than breath to
look down and maybe see
the possible

Yarkon River, fringed with eucalypti
and the boats for rent and the wooden
benches, scratched and peeling.

Translated by Catherine Harnett Shaw

Time Zones

My heart is in the East
and I am at the end of the West.

Yehuda Halevi

1.
As if among traffic signs we move
uncertainly. Will it rain?
Will the price of gas skyrocket?
That letter. Will it arrive in the next mail?
What about polar caps? Will they continue
to melt? In this alien morning
even the face in the shaving mirror
might be an imposter, though I recognize
fissures of disappointment converging
on the mouth. Then your voice, confident
and warm, calls to me, not from the end
of the West, but from a few steps away,
with smells of toast and fresh coffee.

2.
Ridges are being crossed. Plains.
The relief maps of our lives—
eucalyptus bark and time zones.

You in the East and I at the end
of the West, are but white canes
in the hands of blind pilgrims, tapping
the code of our hungers on the dank
ribs of two parallel tunnels.

Translated by Elaine Magarrell

Protective Fences

The bus climbs slowly, and I, tired of translating
degrees of cold and hot into degrees of hot and cold,
distances into distances, leaves into leaves,
life into life, with half-closed eyes
fortify myself behind 22 protective fences,
aleph, *bet*, *gimmel* . . .

When the bus triumphantly crests the hill,
snorting a blue wake that widens like Southern slang,
I open my eyes: the poem is basically
finished, spitefully Hebrew, each
of the 22 chiseled right to left, a small
relief map of Israel.

Translated by Laura Fargas

Shampoo

This morning I washed what's left
of my unruly, mideastern hair
with an aloe shampoo. Then
I used a conditioner rich
with coconut. Now, studying myself
in the mirror, I see my hair shining
like new, each strand in place
like a yacht returned to anchor
after sailing a far distance.

Only in the trenches surrounding
the eyes is some activity visible,
some dissatisfaction lurking
in the mouth's grooves. Glancing
at my watch I discover it tells
the old, Israeli time.

Translated by Barbara Goldberg

Drought

I snake toward you like cracks
in arid soil,
and even if rain takes pity
I'll never be repaired.
Your face becomes conjecture
like the landscape of the moon.
Where do I begin
to map this wilderness?

Translated by Catherine Harnett Shaw

Palma Plicatae[1]

Blessed art thou, creator of tongues: now
when I set forth to explore those ravines, dark in the shade
of their honeyed bushes, this antique language,
ennobled by science and time, serves me well
as I conceal my aim. My passion
is the only existing map, and who
in the name of linguists everywhere
will be smart enough to crack the code?
Ah, the folds! Let me smooth
every one of them with the tongue of my lust,
the winding ruts where groundwater gathers,
wet and sweet in the midst of this heat.

Translated by Catherine Harnett Shaw

---

[1]Folds of the pudenda.

The Art of Waiting

Between Indian summer and the great
snowfall, between the harbinger redbreast
and the last acorn, you and I study the art
of waiting. Strange how time invades
our flesh; strange how our brittle bones
take on a copper hue; we no longer rise
to our toes when metal birds fly overhead.
Truly the flip side to the art of waiting
is the awareness that even on foreign
ground, laws of gravity hold.

Translated by Barbara Goldberg

Trees

Even the trees
in their nakedness,
in their grooves, knots, roots,
store the fragrance
of future flowering.
We are like two
naked trees, stretching
bare hands like branches
to a cold metallic sky
emptied of birds
and only we
know how April
preserves itself
in this stripped forest
where I hold your scent
and you, mine.

Translated by Barbara Goldberg

Marco Polo I

Your scent, an aroma of snow and pine,
drifted up from the open envelope.
And you, dreamer, what voyage did you embark upon?
There was a time when bold men sailed
fragile ships to discover unknown lands,
and along the paths of the steppe
leisurely caravans made their way
among remote people, in search of perfect silk.
And you, dreamer, what voyage did you embark upon?
As the era's harsh noose tightened around the throat,
up from the open envelope drifted your scent,
an aroma of snow and pine.

Translated by Henry Taylor

Marco Polo II

"Tenderly she took my right hand
and held it to her left breast."

Heroic nations decayed in flesh and spirit,
bowed and left the stage. Frontiers
vanished like smoke in wind, blood-red suns
cooled and turned blue. Rivers ran
with filth, grass dried and yellowed.
Weird cries erupted from deep recesses of time.
Yet if only my fingers had moved downward
slightly, they would have found her heartbeat.

Translated by Henry Taylor

Distance

I stretch my arm
and strain and strain
but cannot touch you.
You are so far away.

Yet I ask for the impossible:
that you touch me even if
every flight-stretched vein bursts open,
that you hear my heart through
the din of the world.

Perhaps war will break out tomorrow.
I want you to see my dark eyes
etched on your window-pane
when you return from work tonight.

Translated by Catherine Harnett Shaw

The Meteorologist

The meteorologist forecasts a shift
in the jet stream, cold air
flowing from west to east. I see
margosa trees veiling
their wooden souls with violet shades
in this dusk of a spring that came
soft as autumn, and is softening still,
like a woman, her belly
honeyed by memories of love.

Translated by Laura Fargas

Navigation

Swallows, wild geese, herons go
to the south, driven by orderly urges to survive,
the deepening cold, the changing colors of their blood.
We scatter everywhere, mechanical birds
whose interior navigator went wrong, vanquished
by sudden wanderlust and electric surges.
Swallows, wild geese, herons pass
woods and wetlands, familiar
landmarks; birds greet the air currents
like old friends, calling, honking,
"We are coming! We are coming!"
And what of us? Where are we, where
do we set our faces? What scorches
our throats when we try to give voice
to the simplest words:
love, hunger, life?

Translated by Henry Taylor

Honni[1]

Today I'm still under the spell
of seven hours' jet lag, so that facing
the Japanese cherry tree, her profuse
blossoms, is like glimpsing a bride
through her veil. She stands, virginal
and shy on the banks of the Potomac—
brutal, green-eyed beneath the arrogant
arch of its bridges. This morning
I woke shrouded in fog, unable to tell
if that prolonged wail came from child
or bird or Honni himself, wrenched
from his enchanted sleep under a gnarled
Israeli carob tree, and hurled by a warp
in time to this foreign soil, beyond
the ken of seven hours or seventy years.

Translated by Barbara Goldberg

---

[1]Honni was a legendary rabbi who fell asleep only to wake up seventy years later to find the world completely changed.

Citizen of the World

First we talked about war and peace and how
power corrupts and what's good for the nation.
Then Baba washed her hair. Suddenly I knew
as she dried it, as the hair drier whooshed,
that I don't give a fig for politics, but only
that ease that lets me watch Baba drying
her hair, as if time had no measure and she
was the world's sole custodian, no borders,
no customs officials, and I'm there, sheltered
in the shadow of her hair, in the thick of it.

Translated by Barbara Goldberg

At This Moment

Now, at this very moment, powerful
people convene in sanctums, decide
the destinies of other people, perhaps
even yours and mine.

And I am completely enthralled
by that lovely combination
of your pink woollen socks
and black suede flats.

How can I be so self-absorbed?
Not one cloud in the autumnal sky.
Spruce trees sway. When you lean
back your calf flashes above
a pink sock. Soon I'll touch it.

Translated by Barbara Goldberg

Decision

The Chief of Staff had already decided where
the troops should move, how, and when.
Only I am unable to make up my mind—
whether to bite the lobe
of your left ear
or your right.

Translated by Seymour Mayne

Juniper

For he shall be like the juniper in the desert . . .

Jeremiah 17:6

Leaning on the wooden parapet of the Japanese
tea house you rub juniper needles
and hold them close to my nose.

The cool autumnal noon grays over
the botanical garden and the sharp scent
pinches my nostrils and clings to your fingers.

Then like an ancient queen you fling
crushed needles, like used-up lives, onto
the water of the man-made pond.

Loneliness is now too heavy a burden
among those beautiful, pampered, square-shaped
plots, whose memory holds not even a hint
of some prophetic desert in all their bloom.

Translated by Catherine Harnett Shaw

Connected Vessels

Was the tree whose still-dense leaves sheltered us
a beech, a maple, an oak? You know, we urbanites
are not familiar with the names of trees.
I clung to you as if the sudden
rain was not a simple harbinger of coming cold,
but an expression of God's impatience, his
need to flood. Anyway, complaining
that the rain would ruin your hair, you
didn't sense that at that moment,
somewhere hidden, somewhere secret,
the world's destiny and all its multitudes
hung possibly in the balance. I confess, my selfishness
made me sink my face in your damp hair. I don't know how long
we stood that way, connected vessels in a universe
darkening toward an end, or a beginning.
We might have stayed like that, poured into each other,
if a bolt of lightning hadn't scorched
the arched horizon, the expected thunder
following. You shuddered. Something broke. Running
to the car, we were already separate, and later
when I asked, "Which tree was that?" it seemed that
your indifferent shrug was full of insult, hostile:
you know, we urbanites are not
familiar with the names of trees.

Translated by Catherine Harnett Shaw

Omens

Hadn't I already warned you that something
would happen? In the canal a tortoise thrust
its head through green opaque water; a squirrel
zigzagged across a path; two bicyclers
pedaled by, immersed in the cult
of their youth. Do you really need
more omens? When I clasped your fingers
they were warm; in vain the tallest trees
strained to reach the sky; the market
remained stable. Do you still believe
salamanders are immune to fire?

Translated by Catherine Harnett Shaw

This Alien Light

This alien light bathing my eyes
with oblivion. September. Aircraft
carve permanent routes in that void
called sky. As do cranes and other
birds defying domestication.

Touch me. I want to believe again
in implacable processes, the just
verdict of history, melting
icecaps, the spiraling stars.

Translated by Barbara Goldberg

Curtain

Baba's coming home.
Painted in camouflage colors, the curtain plays
war games with the breeze.
Baba's come home.
Now the world has also vanished
and with a drawn out soft groan something new
—like the distant burst of a sun or shell—
is being born through the slats of the shutter.

Translated by Seymour Mayne

Before Sleep

1.

Before sleep Baba arranges extra
blankets on her feet. "The weight,"
she explains, "will keep me
from flying." Walnut trees
hold still in the garden.

2.

Baba sleeps, her cheek pressed
to the pillow, her hair flowing.
In the garden walnut trees
turn silvery.

3.

In silence I shall steal
to her bedside, dismantle
the burdens of her life, then turn
my back and tiptoe away. Baba
is flying, above walnut trees, above
wandering souls. She soars
higher than milky ways and choirs
of seraphim. When she returns,
her hair will be heavy
with the dust of stars.

Translated by Barbara Goldberg

When You Are Asleep

When you are asleep you are a little girl
who has no bad dreams. Only the silver
glimmering in your hair reminds one
of unspeakable distances. With your eyes
closed you drift from between my arms.
And then from memory.
My palm is so empty, like a death
robbed of its own dreaming.

Translated by Barbara Goldberg

Magnets

That night we heard the rustle of falling acorns
and twigs breaking in the deep, lost forest
where Bluebeard roams with that
bitch, Life, and we were amazed
at our sudden, acute hearing.

And at dawn, deer silently emerged
from among the oaks and studied us
with dark, moist eyes, as if
we had not escaped at all
from the terrible cities of man.

If later we cleaved more fiercely
to each other, it was not because we hungered
to be one with nature, or to return
to the garden, but because our two solitudes
are magnets that among all the matter
in the world have no choice
but to draw each other near.

Translated by Catherine Harnett Shaw

Earth

The maple reddened overnight,
and in the misty dawn, primeval fathers
pleaded with us in the voice of migratory birds
to hurry, leave for southern towns.

Imprisoned by sleep, you moan and grope
for the edge of the lost blanket,
as if for the dream of our summer, gone.

No, it will not be I traversing the brambles of your sleep
to lead the caravan.

Earth is stronger.

Translated by Catherine Harnett Shaw

New Alphabet

Then, when lips refused and the tongue
froze, when the throat burned yet was not
consumed, even one syllable words wore
faces of demons, fled beyond mountains and seas
with the cunning of demons. Can a child
who is slow of tongue and with no
holy mission defy demons?

Still dark. A frail moon crowns
my head. I breathe effortlessly
and lead an infinite column
of words, all clearly enunciated
and shimmering, like white vapors
before the crack of dawn. Sun,
do not rise lest they fade away.

Writing would have been easier, or
the feel of flesh on flesh. And yet
not by divine decree, nor in six
working days, but by struggling
my whole life for this—to create
the alphabet anew so that I
may utter now to you, *Beloved*.

Translated by Barbara Goldberg

Basic Vocabulary

The Inuit, at home in the eternal ice, have thirty
words for snow to tell its shape, its hues,
the taste of it, its sounds.

I'm thinking now, in the hushed glow of the evening lamp,
still gasping, sweat gleaming
on my upper lip, the shadows blue

under your eyes, how
the old miner I've become refuses
to give up, stripping layer

after layer of this clumsy language off, to excavate
that single word and then exhale it, warm
into the dark, that place between your breasts.

Translated by Catherine Harnett Shaw

We Should Give Thanks

Now, after love, you and I relearn
the fundamental landscape, a naïve
painting that is nothing more
than it appears—railroad, pine grove, water tank,
the irrelevance of literature. Soon
the proper aesthetic distance will
assert itself and we'll describe
those shivers and moans. Meanwhile
let us gaze out the window at the October
sunset, and the end of another
luminous day. We should give thanks
for small favors: here comes that old
engine driver, the moon, hauling her cargo
of stars across the vast prairie of sky.

Translated by Barbara Goldberg

Bruise

That bruise my teeth made
on your breast, just
below the left nipple,
won't last. Yesterday
it was dark blue. Today
it is paler. Tomorrow
it will grow even paler.
The day after tomorrow
it will fade away. I told you,
no covenants are eternal.

The leaves of that maple
across the street,
on the traffic island
opposite our house, yesterday
they were dark green. Today
they are sprinkled with red.
Tomorrow they will turn
even redder. The day after
tomorrow they might fall. We knew
summer's sway is not forever.

At the proscribed hour, boats
sail out to sea, planes take off
when the control tower gives
the word. I think tomorrow,
surely by the day after,
the signal to return will come
from the drowned motherland.

Translated by Barbara Goldberg

Ecology

Rain forests are being cut down.
Blue-green shadows coil around
my face like anacondas. Ecology
disrupted: global catastrophe.
And what shall I do? What shall I do?

Love me, I beg of you, a blue-
green shadow from the rain forest.
Love my shiny rubber leaves, now
shriveling from lack of water.
Love the inflamed jaguar eyes,
irises paling. Love the supple
flesh even as it erodes.

This is the last supplication
from the rain forest, the last
warning to you, cruel ecology.
I am the tapir, herbivorous, skirting
the fringe of your life, with a trunk
for a nose and hooves sprouting
from toes. Or maybe I've turned
into a wart hog, or elephant, or
some other species on the brink
of extinction. And what shall I do?

What shall I do?

Translated by Barbara Goldberg

Political Poem

This is
a political poem.

The bitter winter has arrived,
closing in on us.

And in spite of all that,
this worn down body
wants to love you
and revel in its love.

If it is censored
insurrection will break out.

Translated by Catherine Harnett Shaw

Twilight

Twilight bandages our eyes,
a blindfold before the last
order, and all around a silent
world totters and slumps,
its shape altered.

You are the one to know: this
is a late afternoon love, an interval,
while in the distance morning
speaks, its voice not quite
distinct, and night has yet to arrive
with its fiery consummation.

Please now, hold my hand
gently, with great care.

Translated by Barbara Goldberg

Through the Glass Bottom

Time and space cannot vouch
even for themselves. Eternal summer
shrank back ashamed before
a startling winter storm, though
the golden boys and girls still lay
on the shore, scattered like oranges
that ripened and fell, their fingers
spread wide in supplication. Hoping
to hoard time like a chunk of amber,
even in yellowed newspaper, you move
from place to place like a tourist
avid to see the sights, harkening to
a melody of mermaids dying far at sea:
the glass bottom magnifies fish and corals
much beyond their natural measures,
and in the sea's beds, love and life
split and flow together with shifting
currents, not of themselves.

Translated by Laura Fargas

Love and Other Calamities

A scarlet sun, swollen like
a bruised eyeball behind a patch
of damp haze. Even the old don't
remember such unrelenting heat.

But at your house the air-conditioning smooths out
all wrinkles. When the guests arrived we
had already shelved the tiny pains, the day's anxieties,
and with cool, friendly faces, took the opportunity

to discuss global warming, the hole in the ozone layer,
polluted air, the greenhouse effect. After they left,
we exchanged our gossipy impressions, washed the dishes, yawned
behind the backs of our hands. When the summer
storm erupted, it found us
well-prepared for torrential rains, drought,
doomsday, love and other calamities
which the weathermen sometimes forecast
and sometimes entirely miss.

Translated by Catherine Harnett Shaw

Resignation

When friends depart the pressure
in the chest subsides. Once a sun
ripened and burst, squirting seeds
of light straight into the eyes.

The chest still opposes. The history
of light is the body's story, which is,
in turn, the history of a bursting sun.
All eyes are scorched. Friends, departing,

take with them a portion of friendship
to show the way and leave a diminished
light, a small weight in the chest.

What burns the eyes is the memory
of sun. When the chest stops opposing
the weight is lifted. The chill in the eyes
will turn to frost when friendship runs out.

It will be colder, I am certain.

Translated by Elaine Mazarrell

Forecast

The weatherman forecast a storm
for tomorrow: today will still be clear.
As his calm voice talked
about the inevitable, warm sunlight
gilded the windowpane and the poplars'
tranquil leaves. Tomorrow
something will happen. Not today.
The abyss of time between now and then
extends as far as one can see and is
sprinkled with warm gold, a canopy of poplars
sheltering it from all possible storms.

Translated by Elaine Magarrell

Impending Storm

The storm draws near and we are alone
on the deck of this creaking house.
Before we set sail, soothsayers read us
the signs; nevertheless, we raised anchor.
Now the sky has lowered and weighs over
our heads and the sea is opaque like the eye
of a dead fish. As in old yarns, I bind
myself to the tilting helm, and you
like a tired bird, nestle against
my throbbing, human heart.

Translated by Barbara Goldberg

Russian Doll

You are out. The house is quiet as a Trappist monastery.
Above the TV, colored in folkloric lacquer,
a Russian doll displays her wooden smile.
Through the chinks of the curtain a pale spot of light
filters in, falls on the Slavic face
like drops of holy oil. Stealthily looking
around like a spy set to pull photos
out of hiding, I take it off the shelf, dismember
its torso, and from out of the gaping obscene belly,
pull doll after doll, doll out of doll, each
smaller than the other, each identical
to the other, my life varnished in lacquer
with a neutral smile. From whom do they hide?
Why do they masquerade, disguising love
and hatred, making desire and failure uniform
with glowing layers of paint? And why do they grow
incessantly smaller, sperm cells swimming toward
a wooden womb doomed to be barren till the end
of all desire? Returning home, you find the doll
back in place, its multiple selves like an underground
within an underground, its smile betraying
nothing. When you go to the curtain
and with a practiced hand draw its wings
together for harmony's sake, the light
is wiped out as if by a rag. Only the questions
remain. And suddenly appearing in folkloric colors
on my face, a dispassionate, lacquered smile.

Translated by Seymour Mayne

Parting and Demons

Parting breeds demons:
a bear with the head of a bird,
a bird with a goat's legs,
a goat with a lion's paws.
It's difficult to see them in the light.
At night they lie at the foot of the bed,
weeping, afraid of the dark, and lonely.

When you finally arrive from the cement
prairie, dusk has already fallen.
If you look closely, you see them squatting
at the foot of the made bed, surrealistic and ungainly.

You softly place your hands on
their savage heads. Something almost
human flickers in their eyes as they melt away even
in the lightless room, perhaps consoled.

Translated by Catherine Harnett Shaw

Orangutan

Hairy, auburn, the orangutan braces his back
against the stone wall, and with his human fingers
plucks a bunch of grasses. Stem after stem
he brings them to his mouth, delicately
as a deposed prince who has retained only
his good manners. Then he stops feeding
a moment, fixing his eyes on some middle distance.
This removes him from the pit and the fence

dividing us. What thoughts cross his mind,
being so exposed to our vulgar curiosity?
Born in captivity, he cannot cling to the forest
memories, and on all sides impatient America,
which holds no brief for the abstract, muscles in
on him. There now, he returns to his grasses.

Indeed, it's a fit topic of conversation for some
leisure hour. He goes on sitting, hirsute, reddish-brown,
back to the stone wall—a well-defined boundary
to fantasies—nobly crunching his stems, retreating
with an ironical perseverance to what we have
in common. A sudden shame makes us rush to the exit gate.

Translated by Elaine Magarrell

Transfiguration

Last night you said, Look,
a hazy halo around the moon, the sign
for snow. From under the brim
of a black felt hat, your eyes
gleamed like a she-wolf's. Later
in bed you howled and scratched
my back until you drew blood.

Today snow fell on brick houses,
traffic islands, bronze horsemen,
brokers on their way to lunch, the homeless
shuffling to the metro for shelter.
It fell, white and impartial.

You come home from the office
to a picture postcard landscape
already grown dark, your fur boots
tracking silent prints in the snow.
When you shed your gloves, your fingers
are soft and warm, the nails neatly
trimmed, tame as they touch.

Translated by Barbara Goldberg

Tell Me the Truth

Tell me the truth, this acting
like a dog, mournful looks, random
nuzzlings against a breast, thigh, buttock,
haven't you had enough? After all, age
imposes certain limits. A little rest
can't hurt. And the sounds, foreign,
guttural, grunts at the most intimate
moments, surely they jar. Tell me
the truth, aren't you bored? Begging
your pardon, did you say something? Your eyes,
why are they moist? And why do you sprawl
on the couch in that fetching position, excuse me,
in its submissiveness, somewhat doggy?

Translated by Barbara Goldberg

Squirrel

The squirrel zips up and down the oak,
hiding, for squirrely days to come,
a treasure of acorns and nuts, while under
a sky as sweet as a song of salvation,
people both dark and fair
trot back and forth on the roads of time.

Little brother, in the hollows of many trees—
even if none of your local oaks—
I too have stashed, to no avail, acorns and nuts:
when the snow comes, as it will to even the farthest place,
time will smooth all colors into a frieze
merging squirrels and people.

Translated by Laura Fargas

The Changing Season

Maple leaves fall
according to the law
of seasons. We cross over
to the traffic island
and a brisk wind nips
our exposed flesh.

Tonight sniff me out
like a dog hunting
for home. With my arms
outstretched, I'll have lost
all notion of east and west.
Maybe I've changed too,
the features of my face,
the ingredients of my blood,
the dream where you and I
set out for a receding
horizon under icy stars.

Translated by Barbara Goldberg

Delicately

Then said Samuel, Bring ye hither to me Agag the King of the Amalekites. And Agag came to him delicately.

1 Samuel 15:32

In the morning we walked along shady forest paths,
identifying plants not by the guidebook
but by whatever pleased our hearts.
The pines' perfume imprisoned us from every side,
we, willing captives,
like once, in the hills of Jerusalem,
where you have never wandered.

But that night an alien, mincing
summer rain pattered,
like Agag walking delicately
to his death.

Translated by Catherine Harnett Shaw

December

A night made of glass.
Outside, a full moon, milky
as a cataract. Once
on such a night, somnambulists,
midnight martyrs, ascended
to the roofs, their bare feet
staining the ice with blood.

What more is left? Immersed
in dream, the clenched fist
doesn't uncurl. Faces of those
most familiar to us fall
like maculate leaves. On the pillow
your profile suddenly turns
to that of a she-wolf.

Is there time? Is it still possible
to plead for mercy?
On this night, at this house,
angels will remain aloof.

Translated by Barbara Goldberg

Anti-Abstract Poem

The pain of the world is abstract.
Not your pain.
The horror of the world is abstract.
Not your horror.
Traveler among stars,
pick up a handful
of this country's soil.
The faces outside
the window recede
along with the street racket.
Your orphan's moan
rips open the poem's throat.
Your face bleeds
on the scatter rug.

Translated by Barbara Goldberg

Change

Stone is stone.
Tree is tree.
Man is man.

Stone crumbles.
Trees wither.
Man turns again to dust.

Only in the particle of time
my flesh and yours unite
does something change:

scattered stones cleave to stone,
sap bubbles in dry trees,
earth sprouts man.

Translated by Elaine Magarrell

Imaginary Voyages

Now it can be told: we only followed
the heart's directives. Yet they were more
real than any path leading out
from the city's gates. Our boats
sailed farther than fleets of great
maritime nations, cast anchor
at islands where trees bore fruit
more exotic than any science
could have invented; our caravans
carved routes beyond those to China
or India, winding instead to the Mountains
of Darkness and the Sambation.[1]
Not for us to define truth and fiction—
that's for philosophers to debate
in smokey symposia. What we can
affirm is that in our journeys
we found the unicorn and dragon to be
absolutely real, that when our captain
seized the helm, his veins swelled
and grew blue under his sun-scorched
skin, that when our caravan guide
summoned camels at dawn with a call
sharp as a hawk's, they rose in air
that was cool and scented with cinnamon.

Translated by Barbara Goldberg

---

[1]The Sambation is a legendary river, spewing stones on
weekdays and resting on the Sabbath, beyond which dwell
the Ten Tribes of Israel.

Coming Back

When bells toll the last of summer,
the abbot, old Harmonius,
stores in the wrinkles of his face
sun and the scent of lemons.
Presently the scholars will return
to the holy books, delicately spreading
the great pages whose leather binding
shields a reader from heresy.

We also will come back
from the salt steppes and dry pools,
shed the shirts of hair and time,
and with hungry fingers
learn once more our basic braille,
fragrant with sun and lemon scents,
ringing with the voices of small bells.

Translated by Laura Fargas

Imperial Anxieties

Qin Shi Huang Di,[1] which did you
fear most—barbarians in the north
or books written before your time?
You commanded the Great Wall into being
and ordered the ancient texts burnt.
Did you hope to keep not only
massacre and plunder but every foreign
turmoil away from the Middle Kingdom's
tranquility? Or did you try
to erase all wisdoms born before you,
all beauty before the dawns and
dusks of your own eyes, also to spare
your people the great nostalgias
of all wisdom and difference?
We don't know. We only know
the Wall went up with infinite
labor along the northern border
and that the flames rose everywhere
to eat the scrolls, reflecting
like copper butterflies in the waters
of the Yellow and all other rivers.
We know too that the barbarians
did come, their ponies' hooves
staining the fertile land of the South,
and we know that the ashen books
had already been saved in many
memories, that even before
the cinders dispersed, voices
were sharing fragments of stories,

---

[1]As rendered in the now favored Pinyin system.

poems, the monkey fables.
So what, old man, can a king
achieve? On the Great Wall of China,
children of barbarians even
more foreign than the horsemen
of the grassy northern steppes
chase each other up and down
the towers, embrasures, battlements,
and I have found the history of
an emperor and his anxieties
recorded in a book written during
the dawns and dusks of my eyes,
not yours. And, Qin Shi Huang Di,
I may cluck my tongue and go on
reading, or let your story fall
from my hand with disbelief.

Translated by Laura Fargas

150

Identifying Marks

Constantine, last Emperor of Byzantium,
slaughtered when the Turks stormed
Constantinople, was identified
among the corpses by the imperial
purple sandals on his feet.

How long could his capital have withstood
the siege? Its granaries were overflowing;
its walls might have borne the impact
of Turkish cannonballs (more powerful
than ever); and buzzing throughout the streets,
the rumor of rescue by Italian ships,
now that the rift between the churches
of Greece and Rome had been mended.

How to explain the Metropolis' fall?
What of granaries, walls, and rumor
turning amber under an almost
Mediterranean sun? Historians say
one small gate was left unlatched, perhaps
a simple oversight. Through that gate
the Sultan's forces penetrated the city.

I think of that now, here, on foreign soil,
on these bitter winter days so soon
to grow dark, and of the last dead
emperor, his purple sandals, his feet.

Translated by Barbara Goldberg

Circe

An outgrowth of the Mediterranean, the Aegean Sea is home
to Circe who changes men, sometimes into wolves
and leopards, more often into swine. Her dark hair
pours over her white shoulders as she stands,
a monarch facing a wine-dark sea.

And what if those wallowing in the dunghill,
rooting for acorns in the sticky mud, dreamed
of heroes sailing through waves of dark wine,
the ship's prow cutting toward the Golden Fleece?
And what if the wild beasts yearned for justice
and brotherhood before they grew their fangs and claws?

The Aegean Sea is an outgrowth of the Mediterranean: look,
Circe stands on top of the cliff, holding the shape-changing
scepter, contemplating with her deep, violet eyes
the ever-flowing space, in whose wine-dark
currents the ships row on, and sail, and some
go down with bold men holding deep in flesh and bone
the ancient days of metamorphosis and betrayal.

Translated by Henry Taylor

Aliens

The grass is mowed like Samson's braids;
sweetness of dreams thickens the blood
which ghosts along in honeyed skiffs.
Hover—approach, drugged sleep. Tenderly
Delila's strong fingers smooth on sun
lotion, stirring up scents of grass,
so the blunted nerves can never feel
the aliens' invasion, earth and love
changing beyond pity, beyond return.

Translated by Elaine Magarrell

Seeds

Coming home, my friend spoke lyrically
of the narrow streets of Hampstead washed
by soft continuous rain, and of blue
plaques marking historical houses
where famous people lived,
including poets. Listening, I glimpsed,
among tall buildings and hotels,
slashes of the Mediterranean flashing blue fire
like glass slivers children turn in the sun,
and I thought, perhaps in time we too will mark the homes
of famous poets. Meanwhile
we have this brilliant autumn shining
on our faces, that handsome, gallant light, sea
breezes and seeds of poems in hard soil
waiting stubbornly for the first hint of rain.

Translated by Jean Nordhaus

Sap

The Khamsin[1] erupts, taking everyone
by surprise, and out of winter's glassy sky
a crazy sun melts both the expected
and the unexpected in one golden fire.
Around the big conference table, practical
people, taking the balanced view,
flip over their griddle cakes
of well-considered actions lest they be burnt,
and against the window taps the tendril
of a vine still naked and delicate
as a Japanese drawing, the sap
in its arteries already awake
to a golden life of inebriation,
astonishing in its lack of practicality.

Translated by Elaine Magarrell

---

[1]A heat wave.

Reading Poems
at The Red Bar

Schliemann dug in Troy and found
seven cities buried one under the other.
He who digs in The Red Bar will not find
even red under red:
through the windows a woman's shadow
is washing the stairs.

Poets, while you recite, seven Troys
are being raised from soil, ashes,
trash and stones, and through the window
possibly a shadow possibly a woman is washing
stairs no messiah will ever climb: The Red Bar
is entered directly from the street.

Translated by Laura Fargas

Without Commitments

Among the pepper trees the evening breeze
carefully reads each face like braille.

It has no prejudices.
It has no opinions.

If there's a God, He walks here, after another
burning day, slowly, hands clasped
behind His back, very human. A fine pear-
scented fallout is caught in His hair. The evening
breeze leafs His face with cool, careful fingers.

He has no commitments
in this green shade
to either a promised land
or a chosen people.

California, Summer 1990

Translated by Elaine Magarrell

Rag Doll

When Hannah pretends she's "Doctor Hannah," she
miraculously cures all her patients: enough
to place the stethoscope but once and the raggedy
doll is free from pain, enough to give but one
shot with the cracked plastic syringe and it is fully
restored to health. Only with me
does Hannah fail utterly—although I laugh
with all my heart, swearing I'm no longer
sick, no, not at all—I peek up and see
myself, shabby, Mediterranean, tossed
on the nearest snowbank like a rag doll
torn beyond repair, or a toy stethoscope
and syringe too damaged to function,
lying out there in the freezing
urban landscape, faded, discarded.

Translated by Seymour Mayne

A Russian Miniature

When the haze thickens, the mirror's frame
grows opaque like an old Russian icon,
and as in a story by Chekhov a woman and a dog
walk gingerly on damp grass without leaving tracks,
strings of water in their hair.
To get rid of life, all you have to do here
is cross a road, then, like a murderer
still fearfully looking around, guilty or
just not sure he did what he did,
bury the past in a thicket of blackberry,
raspberry, or danewort.
Now you retrace your steps,
nod to the neighbors, smile at the landlady,
drop into an armchair with Akhmatova's poems.
And when the brambled earth fades away,
the sun's *auto-da-fé* grows pale, a lonely curl
of smoke—in memory of heretics—
will scorch your nostrils, and possibly
not even that.

Translated by Laura Fargas

Goliath

*And there went out a champion from the camp of the
Philistines . . .*

1 Samuel 17:4

He was bigger than all
his people, in fact, bigger
than all peoples of the Mediterranean
basin. Six cubits and a span.
A veritable giant.

The stone sunk into his forehead,
entering the flesh as a brook
enters a river. The ground
shuddered when he fell, a titan
in a coat of mail and helmet
of brass and greaves of brass
and a gorget of brass, shimmering
like pure flame in harsh light.

And it was good to fall
like that, between Shochoh
and Azekah, a mountain collapsing,
shaking the foundations
of the earth. Imagine him
years later, at some Philistine
nursing home in Gath, Ashdod
or Askelon, his sparse gray beard

flecked with morning porridge,
his eyes vacant, his memory dim—
he barely remembers what happened
in the valley of Elah—an ancient
ridiculous giant, a freak attraction
for do-gooders and sightseers.

No, it was better thus.

Translated by Barbara Goldberg

Crusaders

Deserted like crusaders on a grassy
hill overlooking a hazy sea
we wait for the tarrying ships of succor.
When darkness slips away birds call out
with foreigners' voices, crying garbled
code words. In the grass a wind
from remote provinces goes by. The fishponds
grow golden. Now, in this silence,
night and fate commingle.

Translated by Myra Sklarew

Upstream

In the harbor ships sail in and out
and cast anchor, fluttering
their colors, displaying various
national flags.

"Thalassa! Thalassa!" cried
Xenophon's soldiers at the end of their long
march across the continent.
Their souls, drunken sea-gulls, whirled
high above the cliffs.

Our backs to the estuary,
the veins of our foreheads swollen,
the two of us lay all our strength
into the oar, rowing upstream,
putting more and more distance between us
and the world's noise, smells of salt, tar,
rotting fish.

Surely, before nightfall,
we will reach a pool of sweet water
where reflections of great trees
tremble like memories of drowned ships.

Translated by Henry Taylor

Reflection

In the mirror I am an old man
with good social skills,
shedding faces according
to the necessities of time and space.

But when the sun sets
I know that I am
what I am,
nothing more than what I am
and nothing less.

And precisely like that I'll return
to the hill-top, to the snail-scarred
sand, and there
I'll honey the roots of the great sycamore,
confronting the changing, cantankerous sea.

Translated by Catherine Harnett Shaw

Harbinger

Among the nut trees of the heart
the breeze is tall tonight.
The thudding of artillery has muted
in an expanse starred with expectations.
Harbinger, if your steps draw near,
please linger at the gate:
tonight the breeze blows high
among the nut trees of my heart.

Translated by Laura Fargas

For Those
Who Would Reprove Me
For My Foolishness

Love, be a white flame
between me and the bloodless
ghosts, and you be the one
to close my eyes when I
am drawn into night's fold.

Translated by Barbara Goldberg

About the Author

Moshe Dor, born in Tel Aviv, joined the Hagana as a young man. He served as a correspondent for the Israeli army magazine and later studied political science and history at the universities of Jerusalem and Tel Aviv where he completed his undergraduate work.

He was one of the founding members and editors of the "Likrat" group, which comprised many of the most important Israeli writers of the early 1950s and promulgated the "New Manner" in Israeli writing. He has published some 30 books, including volumes of poetry, collections of children's verse, literary essays, and two books of interviews with foreign and Israeli writers. He has also translated several works by English, American, and Canadian writers into Hebrew. An initial volume of poems in English translation, *Maps of Time*, was published in England in 1978. *Crossing the River: Selected Poems*, Dor's poems in English translation, appeared in 1989 (The Mosaic Press, Canada). He co-edited *The Stones Remember* (The Word Works, 1991), an anthology of contemporary Israeli poets, most of whom had never before been translated. *The Stones Remember* received the Witter Bynner Foundation Award.

Moshe Dor served for 30 years on the editorial board of *Maariv*, one of Israel's most important newspapers. He also served as its literary editor. Dor represented Israel in 1970-1971 at the International Writing Program at the University of Iowa, and he has served on the presidium of the Hebrew Writers' Union and Israel's Press Council. From 1975 to 1977 he was Counselor for Cultural Affairs at the Embassy of Israel in London. In 1987, Dor was the Distinguished Writer-in-Residence at the American University in Washington, D.C. Dor is an Israeli radio and television personality, commenting on literary as well as other issues.

The recipient of many honors, including the Prime Minister's

Award and the Bialik Prize, Israel's top literary award, Dor was elected
President of the Israeli chapter of P.E.N.

Published Works

Books of Poetry

Broshim Levanim [White cypresses], 1954
Im Nagi'a Ve'im Lo Nagi'a [If we do and if we don't], 1957
Tzav Ikkul [Writ of attachment], 1960
Ma'avar Khatzia [Street crossing], 1962
Zahav Va'effer: Shirei Paris [Gold and ashes: poems of Paris], 1963
Sirpad Umatechet [Nettle and metal], 1965
Icarus Ha'olam [Icarus the world], 1966
Baron Porcelli bi'Yerushalayim [Baron Porcelli in Jerusalem], 1968
Mivkhar Shirim [Selected poems], 1970
Mapot Hazman [Maps of time], 1975
Afifonim Be'Hampstead Heath [Kites on Hampstead Heath], 1980
Ukhvar Ba'hatchala [From the outset], 1985
Berosh Hashunit: Mivkhar Shirim [On top of the cliff: selected poems],
    1986
Ovrim Et Hana'har [Crossing the river], 1989
Ahava Ush'ar Puranuyot [Love and other calamities], 1993

Children's Poetry

Sfina Mitavlot Shokolad [A boat of chocolate slabs], 1968
Ha'armon Shel Amir [Amir's palace], 1970
Mi Rotze Lihyot Kosem [Who would like to be a wizard], 1975
Yom Ve'od Yom [Day after day], 1986
Mesibat Hayanshuf [The owl's party], 1987

Literary Essays

Kri'ah Rishona, Kri'ah Shniya [Reading and re-reading], 1970

Literary Interviews

Legalot Le'adam Acher [To let other people know], 1974
Meshorerim Einam Ratzim Be'Lehakot [Poets don't run in packs], 1985

Translations into Hebrew

Otam Panim [The same faces], Anglo-Jewish poetry, 1981
Mevasser Hachalomot [Vanguard of dreams], poems by Seymour Mayne, 1984
Noheg Leyam Hamelach [Driving down to the Dead Sea], poems by Alan Sillitoe, 1986
Tekes Pashut [Simple ceremony], poems by Seymour Mayne, co-translated with Shlomo Vinner, 1990
Arbeh Hadmama [Locust of silence], poems by Seymour Mayne, 1993
Hadavar Hanora Hakarui Ahava [This terrible thing called love], poems by Barbara Goldberg, co-translated with Giora Leshem, 1993
Okhlei He'afar Halavan [Eaters of the white earth], poems by Myra Sklarew, 1994

Translations from the Hebrew

The Burning Bush, in English, an anthology of contemporary Israeli poetry, co-edited with Nathan Zach, 1977
Maps of Time, in English, 1978
En Bij Het Begin [From the outset], in Dutch, 1988
Crossing the River: Selected Poems, in English, 1989
The Stones Remember, in English, an anthology of contemporary Israeli poetry, co-edited with Barbara Goldberg and Giora Leshem, 1991

MOSHE DOR, born in Tel Aviv, is a major figure in contemporary Israeli writing. He has published some 28 books, including volumes of poetry and literary essays. As a young man he joined the Haganah, and later served as military correspondent. Dor has worked as a journalist, and for many years was on the editorial board of *Maariv*, one of Israel's leading newspapers. He has been Counsellor for Cultural Affairs at the Israeli Embassy, London; Distinguished Writer-in-Residence at the American University, Washington, D.C.; and was elected president of Israeli PEN. He has received many honors, including the Prime Minister's Prize and the Bialik Prize, Israel's top literary award. *Khamsin* traces the parallel struggle of a writer's coming of age and the rebirth of the Israeli nation.

"This wilderness. This oasis that is the land of Israel, this sea made in the shape of a harp. These mountains. These stones into which the sun pours its life. And out of which light goes back into the atmosphere. Moshe Dor is made of this land and infuses everything he writes."

—*Myra Sklarew*
from the Preface